T0274078

# THE
# GOOD
# BERRY
# COOKBOOK

# THE
# GOOD
# BERRY
## COOKBOOK

### HARVESTING AND COOKING WILD RICE AND OTHER WILD FOODS

## TASHIA HART

MINNESOTA
HISTORICAL
SOCIETY PRESS

The publication of this book was supported though a generous grant from the June D. Holmquist Publications and Research Fund.

Unless otherwise indicated by caption or credit, all text and photos copyright © 2021 by Tashia Hart. Other materials copyright © 2021 by the Minnesota Historical Society. All rights reserved. No part of this book may be used or reproduced in any manner whatsoever without written permission except in the case of brief quotations embodied in critical articles and reviews. For information, write to the Minnesota Historical Society Press, 345 Kellogg Blvd. W., St. Paul, MN 55102-1906.

mnhspress.org

The Minnesota Historical Society Press is a member of the Association of University Presses.

Manufactured in the United States of America

10 9 8 7 6 5 4 3 2

∞ The paper used in this publication meets the minimum requirements of the American National Standard for Information Sciences—Permanence for Printed Library Materials, ANSI Z39.48-1984.

International Standard Book Number

ISBN: 978-1-68134-202-3 (paper)

Library of Congress Control Number: 2021938508

## Acknowledgments

I'd like to express my biggest gratitude to my dad, my mom, my grandfather, my uncle, and all the ancestors who lived lives before me and walk with me in mine; all of my friends and colleagues who inspire me; my elders, language teachers, and mentors in culture, art, and science; our youth who are so eager to walk the good path; my ricing partners; the contributors of recipes and stories; the plants, animals, spirits, and Maamaa Aki; with special thanks to Wendy Savage, Vern Northrup, Heid E. Erdrich, Wendy Makoons Geniusz, Shannon Pennefeather, and Jonathan Thunder. This book was supported in part by a Tiwahe Foundation Oyate Network Project Grant (2019), the First Nations Development Institute, and *The Midwesterner*.

Manoomin beds cover the surface of shallow lakes and rivers.

## INTRODUCTION
# Good Berry, Good Food, Good Life

*"We're going to be alright … we're going to be alright … we're going to be alright."*
Manoomin

### Good Berry

There are stories told in our oral traditions of the Seven Fires Prophecy, which foresaw seven eras in the lives of the Anishinaabeg, detailing times of trial as well as opportunity for wellness. In the Seven Fires Prophecy, the people were told to travel westward until they found "the food that grows on the water." Manoomin (wild rice) led our ancestors inland from the East Coast on a journey that took generations. Fueled by faith in their visions and dreams, they encountered the food of prophecy when they reached the Great Lakes region. When our ancestors found manoomin, they knew they were home. And in turn, today our water protectors put their freedom at risk to try to stop the advancement of oil pipelines in watery territories that are the homelands of manoomin. The plants require clean water, just as people do, and a pipeline burst in this delicately balanced ecosystem would wreak havoc for generations to come.

I have found opportunity for wellness in my own life after setting out to develop an intimate relationship with manoomin. The year 2016 was a rough one, and I was in need of guidance. As we do in these times, I put out my asemaa (tobacco) and asked for help. I was instructed that I would find the growth I needed to be a healthier Anishinaabekwe (Anishinaabe woman) by learning more about manoomin. Soon after, I started making elaborate plans to bike across the Great Lakes region to gather stories about manoomin, traveling all the way back to the East Coast. Then, in December 2018, an editor with the Minnesota Historical Society Press contacted me about writing a book on manoomin, developing a cookbook,

In the fall, "rice beards" can turn "manoomin red."

Manoomin makes its home in the shallow waters of lakes and rivers. As a food, it is nutrient dense, notably with protein, fiber, amino acids, and folate. As it reaches the surface of the water, it goes through a "floating stage" before climbing to heights of as much as ten feet. Sitting just above the male flowers, the female flowers hold tight to the stalk while the males fan out, sending their pollen through the wind to fertilize nearby female flowers that are ready before the females of the same stalk, thus cross-pollinating. Manoomin is harvested in late summer and early fall, depending on local yearly conditions.

This poem is inspired by Nookomisiban (my grandmother who has passed away). She was our family's matriarch. She always had open arms, an open house, and an open table. She was a talented cook and baker who worked for the school district we attended on our reservation. My brothers and I would sing a special song about our grandmother and her penchant for feeding us well. On occasion I would hear her singing the song to herself.

### Gramma, Where's the Goodies?

*My grandmother cooks,*
*early in the morning*
*when it's brighter inside*
*than it is*
*out.*
*The birds in their nests,*
*take turns keeping sleepy eyes*
*on the progress*
*of the bubbling*
*berry sauce*
*on the*
*stove.*
*The day is still young*
*and quiet enough*
*that the squirrels can hear her*
*from their drey,*
*as she sings along*
*with the rhythm*
*of her*
*stirring,*
*"Gram-maaaa, where's the goo-dies, goo-dies?"*
*"Gram-maaaa, where's the goo-dies, goo-dies?"*

essentially. The idea seemed like a more realistic, and perhaps safer, way to approach what I had been instructed to do. I knew I needed to take on this project.

The practice of manoominike (harvesting manoomin) has been in the hands of the men in my family for decades. My dad's been at it since 1975. However, not long back, the women did the ricing. For various reasons, there was a shift from women to men being the main harvesting forces in our communities. This shift hasn't happened everywhere, but in communities where it did there's been a movement of women seeking to learn the ways and take their place amid the rice beds. I grew up cleaning and cooking rice, but it wasn't until fall 2020 that I had the experience of manoominike. Manoomin has been with me my whole life, and it feels right to join the women who are reclaiming this tradition. It's as if I'm reclaiming a piece of myself and reclaiming my power.

I've been ricing a few times to date; I'm certainly no expert but definitely a dedicated learner. I have more personal experience with the other plants discussed within these pages. I have been humbled to take on the task of creating recipes that incorporate manoomin in some way, big or small. I grew up eating manoomin with a little butter, salt, and pepper, usually accompanying fish, deer, or partridge, as well as in soups with hominy and wild game. In my exploration for this book, I've come to understand manoomin to be much more versatile than I had imagined. After some basic preparations, manoomin can be incorporated into just about any type of recipe: candy, pies, crackers, beverages, and more. Many of the recipes in this book are baked goods that involve manoomin flour or pudding. My grandmother was a baker, and she inspired my original interest in baking when I was a teenager. Some of the recipes are quick and easy, others will take some time, and a few will require a greater working knowledge of and relationship with plants.

## Good Food

This book is about finding abundance in relationships with the people, places, and environment where you live. It's also an observation about the difference between abundance and excess. Excess (and lots of food waste) is the result of the current mass-scale food production and distribution systems in the United States. And yet so many still go hungry. It seems these systems are best at creating separations between those who can afford as large a portion as they desire and those who cannot afford enough to meet their basic nutritional needs. It's a sad state we're in.

Abundance, as opposed to excess, is something entirely different.

The smell of cleaned manoomin is one that I cherish at any given opportunity. It never fails to send fireworks of life and memory through my nervous system, soothing my emotional landscape, energizing my spirit, softening my heart, and grounding my limbs to a place—this place, the woodlands and waterways of northern Minnesota.

You might be asking: *What is cleaned manoomin?* And, *What is the aroma akin to?* Cleaned manoomin is what you have after much time and effort and before you cook the prepared seed in a pot. Within the smell is a folded abundance: the sunlight that drew the manoomin up to break the water's surface; the excitedness in searching out, of waiting and watching for manoomin while it grows; the life of manoomin on the water in community with other beings; the energy and sweat from the harvest; the wind; the fire and smoke of being parched; and the smell of manoomin powder on my father's hands, a mingling of skin, sunshine, and all that is manoomin—this is how I know this smell best. You have to be a patient smeller to smell these things. Like a patient listener, a patient smeller gains information about action and emotion, a sense of (well-)being. Love lives in the in-betweenness.

Cleaned manoomin

Kevin Hart Jr. checks manoomin for ripeness.

When I discuss Indigenous foods, I'm ultimately talking about relationship. I'm speaking of the foods that have historically nurtured and shaped our bodies, our cultures, and our traditions as Indigenous peoples of this land base we know as Turtle Island from our Anishinaabeg creation stories. Other tribes have different names for this land base. In turn, the history of each of our Indigenous foods is also tied to this land, and to us. Our histories are shared. People, plants, and animals become indigenous to a place via a historical upbringing in a shared space on our Gimaamaanaan Aki, Mother Earth.

*When I was a young woman, I found myself homeless on more than one occasion. I've had an abundance of gratitude for every little thing in my life since.*

There are stories passed down about many if not all of the plants around us. Often our cultural hero Wenabozho (Waynaboozhoo, Nanaboozhoo, Nanabush) is involved. While I have been influenced by these stories, this book is not a retelling of our traditional stories and teachings. When I talk about manoomin or other plants or animals or give any opinions, they are my own, based on my own life lessons. I am one person who only knows what I know. I have limitations; it has taken time to understand what they are, and I now find comfort in knowing they're there. No one is meant to know everything. Understanding this truth is what makes talking to other people— and plants and animals—so rewarding. (We'll get into talking to plants a bit later.)

Hands that smell of all these good things draw in that love—a sustenance, if you will—which is transferred and felt in the passing of food. Passing ricing knowledge from one to another is essentially a passing of access to memories, being, responsibility, and love, all flowing in a movement that transcends physical boundaries, connecting generations—worlds, even.

"Eating manoomin is a by-product," my dad once told me. The more I understand about how the life, harvesting, and care of manoomin is intertwined with our people and how that care shows up in our own lives, the more I understand what he means. Manoominike (harvesting manoomin) is more than just acquiring food. It's deeply rooted in our paradigm of relationships, knowledge, and values. Our identity, you might say, has grown with manoomin. This growth, this identity is what I think of when I think of "good food."

On this note, I have to roll my eyes whenever school-taught propaganda insists "hunter-gatherers" exist(ed) as an earlier stage in human evolution to the modern capitalist paradigm and standards of living. Values and curiosity determine the evolutionary path and type of intelligence fostered. The fact that hunter-gatherers aren't/weren't inventing the next smartphone doesn't mean they aren't/weren't dealing with a vast amount of knowledge on a daily basis. It's a destructive narrative, this alleged evolution from gatherers to farmers to capitalists, a narrative historically tied to Indigenous people being deemed "uncivilized" so that settler colonists could feel less guilt about strategically displacing us from the land. However, we are still here and still practicing traditions, old and new.

## Good Life

I'm from Red Lake, which is a reservation totaling more than 840,000 acres in north-central Minnesota. Our band is also called the Red Lake Band of Chippewa (aka Ojibwe, aka Anishinaabe), and the village on the rez I know best is called Red Lake. We are a band of Anishinaabeg who identify with the lake of the same name that is mostly within the borders of the reservation. Naturally, we are known as Red Lakers.

I come from a family that hunts, fishes, rices, and picks berries and tea. My dad has always been a fisherman, and in the eighties when I was a girl, before netting was forbidden, in the summertime he'd have nets hanging up in "back of town" at my grandma's house. I'd watch him clean nets and sort fish and hear him telling stories with his fisherman friends. I learned to fillet fish by watching him do it hundreds or thousands of times.

My Anishinaabe dad is one of my first mentors. He taught my siblings and me about the plants and animals around us as we grew up in the environments of northern Minnesota. He has always hunted, fished, and harvested with the seasons. Because of him, I developed a deep appreciation for wild foods and places. My father has afforded me the priceless gift of a personal, intimate connection to the landscape. I know that my life force is dependent upon it.

My mother is my other first mentor, a bookworm with Gaelic (among other) ancestry who has always loved to read about medicinal plants from across the globe and put their healing properties into practice. For example, she would calm us with celery seed and numb sore teeth with clove buds and made sure we ate fresh veggies.

I'm thankful that my parents' appreciation for the plant world was combined and seeded into my own.

Many relatives, friends, and community members influence my studies in food, medicine, art, and lifeways that are now called traditional ecological knowledge. My love for the natural world led me to study biology at Bemidji State University, just thirty miles south of Red Lake.

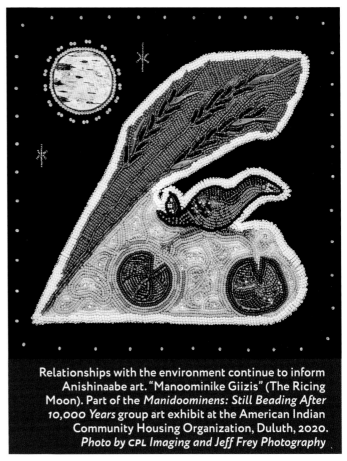

Relationships with the environment continue to inform Anishinaabe art. "Manoominike Giizis" (The Ricing Moon). Part of the *Manidoominens: Still Beading After 10,000 Years* group art exhibit at the American Indian Community Housing Organization, Duluth, 2020. *Photo by CPL Imaging and Jeff Frey Photography*

Red Lake

I grew up eating wild foods, and the older I got and the more I learned, the more I started to plan my year around scouting and harvesting these foods, along with learning about as many new wild foods as I could. Having grown up in poverty, as a young adult I was resourceful; being able to harvest food from the environment was a huge gift. When I really began to see just how much food was around me, I was overcome with a sense of empowerment that has never left me. Food sovereignty *is* empowerment.

I've been known as a "culinary ethnobotanist" since 2016, when my friend, and at the time boss, Sean Sherman deemed me as such as he attempted to describe the role I was playing on the Sioux Chef catering team. I foraged ingredients, handled the baking, traveled to cook at food summits, helped cater events, and led some foraging hikes. While I find this label entertaining, I have always felt that because it is sculpted with a foreign language built on foreign constructs, it could use a little amending. I've racked my brain, wondering how I could more fully describe who and what I am.

I've come to the simple conclusion that I am Anishinaabe. I do my best to learn how to be a better Anishinaabe with every revolution around the sun I'm given. I'm not an elder nor one of the sacred knowledge keepers. They understand things about our origins, the land, the plants and animals, the spirits, the spirit world, and the ways we are connected to one another. A lot of their knowledge is specific to a place. This place. When you add up these things, you can see why our people honor our elders and knowledge keepers and look to them for guidance on how to live a good life in harmony with the rest of creation. They have much to teach us all. Our elders and knowledge keepers are national treasures.

From professors I've learned about the scientific process and certain ways of observing things. For instance, mainstream scientific methods rely on reproducible observations within the natural world to have conclusive evidence for this or that bit of knowledge. In contrast, my plant and animal teachers need not show me the same things twice, for the nature of the teachings are a shift in consciousness that can't be pushed back. However, I do think that developing both hemispheres of my brain, so to speak, has benefited my overall experience as a human being. For example, learning how to recognize botanical structures and the habits of plants in an academic setting has increased my ability to notice and identify plants in the wild.

After graduating college, I spent some time working with my grandfather in the Red Lake Traditional Foods Program in 2012. We would tend to gardens, find locations of wild foods, and create surveys and educational materials for the community to get a better idea of what our needs were and create awareness for healthy eating and lifestyles.

After that I spent about four years making birch bark and beaded jewelry. I first learned to bead in kindergarten on the rez stringing crow beads and later learned to use a loom and make daisy chains. I was inspired by family members who were artists and craftspeople in their own ways, making regalia, beaded jewelry, war clubs, and a variety of other things. As an entrepreneurial jewelry artist in my late twenties and early thirties, I would go to tribal offices, colleges, and community centers on reservations in Minnesota and sell my handmade items. I would also sell off the rez, learning to interact with gift store owners and consign and wholesale my work. I met so many wonderful people who bought my wearable art and really helped boost my self-confidence. I learned about self-reliance during this time.

By 2016 I was collaborating in the Sioux Chef Catering Company kitchen in the Little Earth community in Minneapolis with Sean Sherman, Brian Yazzie, Vern DeFoe, and the Tatanka Truck crew. I learned a lot during that time and carry those teachings with me. I've met Indigenous cooks and environmental caretakers from across Turtle Island, and I'm proud on a daily basis for all the hard work they put into their communities that in turn informs the rest of the world.

Thanks to a variety of life experiences, I now make a living as an all-around creative by incorporating my love of people, plants, animals, and the environment into everything I do: writing children's books and novels, illustrating, creating beadwork, harvesting foods, and providing consultations. I'm also a member of the I-Collective, an autonomous group of Indigenous chefs, activists, herbalists, and seed and knowledge keepers.

You will find a variety of wild plant foods discussed in this book. Most of the recipes are vegetarian and/or vegan. I didn't set out to write a mostly vegetarian cookbook; this collection is simply a reflection of how I like to eat. I eat meat only when my body tells me it is needed—maybe once a week, sometimes less.

When I was a kid and I saw animals suffering it was always very upsetting for me. But I never associated suffering with the wild game my dad brought home. That felt different. I've always loved fish, venison, and partridge, the main proteins he'd bring for our family's sustenance. When I was twelve or thirteen, I realized I didn't have to eat meat if I didn't want to. I chose to follow a vegetarian diet for fourteen years after that. On only one occasion during that time did I eat a bite of salty ham when I was very hungry. Other than that, I didn't eat any kind of meat at all. I felt like I was healing that part of me that had been emotionally distressed from seeing animals suffer.

It wasn't until I was in my mid- to late twenties that I started eating wild proteins again. I think it was venison that I first ate after that fourteen-year break from meat. I was in college, and I had been feeling very tired from running back and forth across campus every day. After I ate that meat, the next day I was bouncing up the steps, amazed at how much energy I had. I knew then that I would occasionally incorporate some meat into my diet.

I prefer wild proteins, but in a pinch I will choose turkey or bison from the grocery store. I've come to accept that this is my way, this is the way I'm made to be, the way I'm meant to see. I don't exclude meat from my diet because I think people are wrong for eating meat. I do it because my body tells me I don't need it and my heart tells me not to perpetuate food systems that exploit animals and cause them harm for profit. I'm not a food shamer. We're all in this together. But I do need to speak my own heart and mind.

I've always been sensitive to the energies of animals as well as humans. People who know me know I like my quietude. As a younger woman, I wondered if I was broken in some way that made it hard for me to be around people for very long. Talking to people in public, especially in crowded urban settings, has always been hard for me. It's challenging to focus on a person's energy when there's a variety of energies flying around everywhere. I've always felt the emotions and energy of other people. I've traced this empathy back to when I was two or three and would try my best to comfort my mother by rubbing her back when I felt she was in emotional pain. I remember being outside of her bedroom, looking through the crack in the door, the bedroom mostly dark, and I could sense my mother's pain like a beacon.

After suffering certain traumas in my teens, my sense of well-being that relied on my emotional body feeling at peace was upset to the extent that I felt like I was in

The ages of sixteen and seventeen were really intense for me. I was trying my hardest to set off on a good path, away from alcohol and harmful relationships. I spent a lot of time meditating, praying, and walking through the woods behind my dad's house on the rez. The plant Indian pipe, also known as ghost pipe (*Monotropa uniflora*), and I came together for the first time then, as I walked along, my arms out, feeling and hearing the pines and soil in the forest. Somehow, those trees sent back waves of knowing, and in the form of images I got the message that what that forest needed were these little white flowers. "Flowers of peace" is how I saw and felt them. I saw them needing to grow in the spaces under the pines, and in my vision I was helping draw them up from the soil. It felt like I had tapped into a big love, helping the earth grow. The next year I found them in physical form growing all in that area. I had never seen that plant before. I was so surprised that I picked one and later that day showed it to my grampa, who told me what it was.

Around the same time, corn revealed itself to me as a part of myself, in a way. I dreamt I was a cornstalk growing in a cornfield; I was a powerful, pure-in-form corn woman. I was holding a baby corn in my arms like a child. I could feel the earth pulsating up and into my parts; we were one and the same. I was so strong. I was the earth. And the corn. And woman with child. Over the years I've met people who have had similar dreams and visions about corn. These earliest two inter-actions with plants had a great impact on my sense of self; I later recognized both as direc-tives leading me to recognize my good path. It seems to be a universal experience, the powerful connections we can have with plants that leave people changed forever.

a mental and emotional prison all the way through my twenties. I had compounded traumas that oscillated and spun the energy of my internal landscape into a night-mare. My own emotional turmoil made experiencing the incoming emotions of other people very confusing for me, and for years I attempted to heal people around me in an effort to heal myself.

I have a lot of thanks to give to the plant and animal beings I discuss within these pages for their role in my successes in healing and fostering self-love and accep-tance. These beings truly make me feel like I belong on this planet. They led me out of depression and continue to soothe my anxious nature. With each season, I wait for them to wake and emerge in their good time so I can greet them. Walking in the woods and forming relationships with plants and animals has always helped me feel safe and at ease, like everything just might be okay. Through the journal entries and stories collected here, my goal is to share a doorway to the peace I've found on my journey and help others have faith in a bright future for their own healing process. My intention is to shine light on spaces we can hold with plants and animals, spaces that nurture our bodies, minds, hearts, voices, and spirits.

This book is many things. Mostly, it is an intimate narra-tive of resilience woven together with practical recipes along with anecdotal "recipes" I've found for cultivating vibrancy and purpose in my own life, seeded by dreams and visions, much in the way of the Anishinaabeg since time immemorial. It is a praise of the plants, animals, water, Earth, and ancestors, and I wrote it for them, along with anyone on a journey of recovering their happy, healthy, whole self. There is room in these pages for home cooks of all levels of experience to explore and grow, with manoomin beside you, shining all that goodness into your kitchen and into your life. Mii minik waa-ikidoyaan, jiibaakwedaa! (That's all I want to say; let's cook!)

White flowers of peace

# Botany Basics

## About the Plants Discussed

While I mention and highlight specific plants in this book, the foraging sections should be used in conjunction with in-person teachings about plant identification and the wild plants in your area, by someone who knows them intimately and can show you what to look for. Some plants discussed in this book have look-alikes that, while not identical, can make it tricky to distinguish the differences unless you have someone show you firsthand. I want every reader to experience the joys of wild foods and none of the mishaps that occasionally occur from only looking at pictures or reading descriptions. And when you are learning firsthand with a plant guide, be sure to pay close attention and always wait until they tell you everything they have to say about a plant before deciding if you want to stick a portion of it in your mouth. I learned this lesson the hard way.

I once attended a foraging session with a plant guide in the Seattle area while visiting to help cook a dinner for the elders of the Muckleshoot tribe. Out on our hike, I had my first introduction to skunk cabbage. I had seen skunk cabbage in books and had heard about it but had never been shown this plant by someone in person. And in my brief reading I must have missed the part that said, "do not chew the raw leaves of this plant on any account," and I also must not have paid close enough attention to the guide, because I popped a small piece of the leaf in my mouth and chewed it for a few seconds before spitting it out. It wasn't bitter, and I'm so glad I didn't swallow it. For the next half hour my mouth and the back of my throat felt like they were full of little shards of glass. It was a struggle to breathe and the back of my throat felt like it was swelling shut. Thankfully, my throat didn't close all the way. But if I had swallowed that one bite of leaf, it very well might have. People have been known to die from this type of grave error.

Since this incident, I have found this plant abundant in my own region, making me wonder what could've happened had I found it in the wild sooner, when I was overenthusiastic and would sometimes nibble on things willy-nilly. I have not chewed on anything without knowing its identity and the full details about it since, and I have the utmost respect for even the most inconspicuous little green thing growing beneath my feet. It is with humility that I tell you my own reckless account— not to make you fearful but to demonstrate the importance of learning patiently and with a teacher, in person.

## Botanical Terminology

Anishinaabemowin offers an abundance of terms for all things plant. These words have teachings associated with them, as well as a worldview from generations of learning. I am not a fluent speaker and do not assume I know much in this respect. I am a humble learner on a lifelong journey and appreciate all the teachings I receive. I will include some basic words and descriptions here but will not attempt to teach things I do not fully understand. Those teachings are for our elders and knowledge keepers to share.

I have learned over the years that different people have different Ojibwe names for plants that are associated with how they know a plant. Names vary. When someone tells me a name for a plant that is different

Manoomin has grasslike, simple leaves with smooth edges.

from others I may have heard before, I'm thrilled because it means I'm about to learn a new aspect about a multifaceted being. Plants can present themselves in different ways to different people, a fascinating detail that makes sense because one plant can have many special attributes.

While it's not necessary to master a plethora of botanical terminology to learn about plants, knowing a few key things can be really helpful, for example, if you're wanting to look up a plant on the internet or speak about a plant to a person from a different community and be certain that you're both talking about the same plant. The following overview of some botany basics can help inform your exploration and conversation.

### The Growth Habits of Plants

Tree, bush, vine, forb/herb, graminoid: these are some main growth habits of plants that are also common descriptors that help us identify them. Manoomin, for instance, is a graminoid. It does not have a woody stem like trees or bushes. Unlike a vine, it grows without external structural support. The telltale characteristic of a graminoid is a grasslike appearance. Forbs/herbs—for example, milkweed and dandelion—do not look like grass.

### Miinikaanan—Seeds

Brimming with nutrients, seeds provide a special kind of sustenance. Unlike with the fruit of an apple or the leaves of a lettuce, eating a seed essentially transfers the potential to grow an entire plant into your own being. Seeds pair well with manoomin. Try blending cooked manoomin with sauteed sprouted lentils in stir-fries or incorporating sunflower or squash or pumpkin seeds and dried fruit with popped manoomin to make your own trail mixes. A few of the most notable edible wild seeds in Minnesota, which all happen to be nuts, are acorns, hazelnuts, and black walnuts. All three require various degrees of processing before they can be eaten or incorporated into recipes. One could write a whole book on the different acorns and processing methods alone.

The oil of the tiny seeds of the evening primrose, a fairly common wildflower found most often in sunny fields, is used in cosmetics and other applications. Primrose seeds are about 20 percent oil and high in linoleic and omega-6 acids as well as minerals.

All of the types of seeds mentioned above are *dicotyledonous*, giving rise to dicot plants. The seeds of dicot plants have two cotyledons, or embryonic leaves. The leaves of dicots tend to have netlike veins. An example of a *monocotyledonous* seed is a corn kernel, which gives rise to a monocot, the corn plant. Manoomin is also a monocot plant, and the part we eat are the seeds. Monocots typically have long, narrow leaves that look like grass and have parallel leaf veins.

If you ever have the chance to learn from a seed keeper, I urge you to take it. There are so many kinds of seeds, all beautiful in their own life-giving way, and seed keepers tend to have intimate stories about seeds to share.

### Ojiibikan—Roots

A variety of wild edible and medicinal roots grow in Minnesota. Some we might consider roots on first glance are actually underground-growing, lateral stems called *rhizomes*. Cattail and wild ginger both have rhizomes. Foods like potatoes and wild potatoes, also known as hopniss or groundnuts (*Apios americana*), that we also tend to think of as roots are actually modified, starchy stems called tubers. They all grow underground, and it's fine to think of them as being in the same realm as roots, but it's good to know these other terms as well. Like all plants mentioned in this book, these plants

Mitigominan, acorns (see page 128)

Bagaanag, hazelnuts (see page 128)

The edible flowers of evening primrose cling to the stalk in a flower spike.

Developing fruit of evening primrose

require in-person teachings for proper identification, harvesting methods, and lessons on good stewardship.

Taproots, like carrots, are a more commonly eaten type of root. The root of a burdock plant is a good example of a wild taproot. It is an invasive plant, and thankfully for us it is delicious. Burdock root is harvested in the spring and fall. I like to peel and chop the roots, boil them for several minutes, and then panfry them. I first became curious about burdock root after reading Samuel Thayer's foraging guides and suggestions for preparation. Burdock roots have a unique texture and flavor, one I personally appreciate. If you gather them outside of spring or fall, there's a good chance the roots will be spongy and won't cook as well or taste as good.

### Zaagigi—Shoots and Sprouts

Less noticed are the sprouts and shoots of plants. In late spring, as you walk through the woods or along the rivers in Minnesota, your eyes will certainly be joyed to see an abundance of greenery sticking up out of the earth—greenery that might not have many discernable features. These are the shoots and sprouts of plants.

On their way from seed to shoot, plants go through a sprouting stage. No doubt you're familiar with sprouts being offered in most grocery stores and in certain food items in restaurants. But what kind of sprouts? Most likely alfalfa, broccoli, radish, or red clover. Odd that they are sometimes labeled ambiguously as "sprouts," without mention as to what kind, isn't it? This detail might not be worth a second thought, but as a plant fanatic I can't help but wonder about the who, how, when, and where—the details of these "sprouts" and their lives. Mung beans are also a popular sprout, found in chow mein and egg rolls, to name a couple popular dishes containing that type of plant structure.

It should be mentioned that "microgreens" and "baby greens" aren't botanical terms; they're marketing terms. Microgreens refer to young plants from the sprout stage up to the point of being marketable as baby greens. Sprouts and shoots, on the other hand, are botanical terms. Examples of commonly eaten shoots are celery and asparagus. Did you know that none of these common sprouts and shoots are those of plants indigenous to the Americas? This detail might lead someone to ask: *Which edible shoots are indigenous to the Americas? And which ones grow in Minnesota? And which ones grow in my backyard?* Fern fiddleheads (shoots) and common milkweed shoots are two fairly widespread types and are both edible and delicious with the right preparations.

*Monocotyledon* plants (typically) have sprouts that emerge from the seed with one leaf, while *dicotyledons* have two. A *radicle*, the embryonic root and the first structure to emerge from a seed, grows out and then down into the soil. Some sprouts of common foods are in this stage. Plants don't stay in the sprout stage for long, and they tend to be very small: blink and you will miss them. The *epicotyl* (seedling's stem) then grows and sends the plant upward from the ground, giving us the shoot. Shoots refer to the stem structure that is quickly shooting upward away from the ground; it can have leaves and other parts to it. Shoots that are eaten tend to be the young ones that are still tender, having had less time to grow fibrous while also containing the most nutrients. Wild nettle shoots with young leaves are one delicious example. The stems of nettles that were delicate in the spring will become full of tough fibers by the fall, at which point they can be gathered and made into cordage.

The sprouts and shoots of manoomin are special in that they mostly grow underwater. However, there is the chance you might spot some along the muddy shore of a lake experiencing a low water level.

A much younger me, happy with my burdock root harvest

The split, dry dehiscent fruit of evening primrose has many seeds inside waiting to be knocked out by gusting winds.

Dr. Arne Vainio picks nettles in the springtime with gloves on, protecting his hands from the raw plants' sting. *Photo by Ivy Vainio*

Stinging nettle has opposite, simple leaves with sharp-toothed edges and a deeply grooved stem. This end-of-summer plant is almost ready to be harvested for cordage.

### Aniibiishan—Leaves

*B*asal leaves stay at ground level, often forming a rosette (circular arrangement). Examples are those of wild leek, dandelion, pussytoes, and plantain. Plants can have both basal rosettes as well as leaves on their main stems. Often these two types of leaves look much different from one another, even though they're from the same plant. This variety in structure can make you think you're looking at two different plants.

*Opposite* or *alternate* are terms describing how leaves are arranged, whether opposite or alternate of one another (sometimes they are a bit of both). Examples of plants with opposite leaves are stinging nettle, common milkweed, and highbush cranberry. Examples of alternate leaf arrangements are those found on chokecherry, birch, and common yarrow.

*Whorled leaves* whorl around the stem, such as the leaves of the Michigan lily, starflower, and spotted joe-pye weed.

*Simple leaves* are like those of plum trees, birch, common milkweed, maple, bergamot, gooseberry, and chokecherry. Examples of *compound leaves* are ash trees, common yarrow, sumac, many if not all ferns, roses, walnut, and mountain ash. Compound leaves can look like leaves on top of leaves, with leaflets making up each bigger individual leaf, while simple leaves are just that: simple, every leaf attached to the main stem or branch.

The leaves of manoomin are basal, alternate, and simple.

### Waabigwaniin—Flowers

*F*lowers are some of the most eye-catching features certain groups of plants have and might be one of the first things you notice about them. You'll probably notice the size and color of a flower, and maybe the smell, if there is one. And when you look a little closer still, you will notice differences in the small parts that make up flowers—the number of petals and presence or lack of other small parts. It's helpful to be able to identify these little parts, to then be able to tell the difference, with the help of other features, between plants that at first glance can appear very similar. Monocots have flowers with parts in multiples of three, while dicots typically have flowers with parts in multiples of four or five.

Not all plants have flowers. Whether a plant has flowers or not is one of the first distinctions you might be able to make. However, this assessment can be tricky if, for example, you're looking at a large maple tree that's past its flowering stage or pondering a vine that seems to come from nowhere and goes somewhere and there are no flowers to be seen on it. And pine trees, for example, bear cones that give rise to seeds, without ever having flowers come into play.

*Angiosperm* is the term for a flowering plant, and angiosperms represent the majority of plant species. *Perfect flowers* have both male and female structures on a single flower. *Imperfect flowers* have either male or female structures (see manoomin flowers, page 21). *Pistillate flowers* have only female structures: stigma(s), style(s), ovary(s), and ovule(s). The stigma captures pollen, and the ovule is what turns into a seed. The ovaries, when swollen, are fruit. *Staminate flowers* have only male structures: the stamen(s), which consists of filament(s) and anther(s). The anther is where the pollen is made; the pollen is where the sperm are.

Regardless of flower type, the pollen and sperm must make their way to an ovary by means of a stigma, whether on the same flower on the same plant or a different flower on the same plant or a flower on a different plant altogether. Requirements for pollination vary for each species, and pollination can be carried out in a variety of ways: by gravity, wind, or water or with the help of insects and other pollinators.

Manoomin plants growing in a muddy shore

# Aniibiishan—Leaves

The basal leaves of wild leek are reddish in color near the ground.

Common milkweed has simple, oppositely arranged leaves.

Chokecherry has simple, alternate leaves.

Michigan lily has a whorled leaf arrangement.

Gooseberry leaves are simple and usually palmate (looking like the palm of your hand), with lobes spreading outward.

Sumac leaves are divided and composed of leaflets. The leaves are compound and alternate.

Yarrow has compound leaves.

# Waabigwaniin—Flowers

Blue flag irises are monocots and have flower parts in multiples of three.

Rose flowers have ovaries as well as pollen, as shown here on the tips of the many yellow anthers of this wild rose.

Butterflyweed is a dicot and has flower parts in multiples of five.

Staminate flowers of manoomin growing below the pistillate flowers clinging tightly to the stalk

Many species of wild violets are edible.

Wild rose petals going into the dehydrator for later use in tea, rose water, and sauce

Monoecious flowering plants have both pistillate (female) and staminate (male) flowers on one plant. *Dioecious* flowering plants have their male and female flowers on entirely separate plants.

Manoomin is an angiosperm, a monoecious flowering plant, with imperfect, separate pistillate and staminate flowers on each plant. The staminate flowers grow beneath the pistillate flowers on the stem.

### Fruit

Fruits are the ovaries of plants. They can be fleshy or dry. If dry, they are *dehiscent* or *indehiscent*, referring to whether they burst open or not as a mechanism to disperse seeds. Fleshy fruits are the fruits we often include in our diets: peaches, apples, cherries, and grapes. Some of the common vegetables we eat are also technically fruits (although not necessarily fleshy): pea pods, green beans, tomatoes, squash, zucchini, peppers, and so on. Some wild edible fleshy fruits found in Minnesota include blueberries, ground cherries, and plums. Examples of dry dehiscent fruits sold in grocery stores are legumes, and a wild example is the common milkweed pod. Both will eventually dry and burst open to disperse the seeds within.

*Zizania palustris*, aka the manoomin plant, has dry, indehiscent fruits called *caryopses*, typical of grasses. The caryopses require threshing or jigging (dancing on the rice) to remove the fibrous, dry outer layer (composed of the *pericarp*—ripened ovary wall—fused with the seed coat) before we can cook it.

I love including flowers in my diet. However, I am very reserved when it comes to eating more than a few here and there, as I know that for every flower I eat, there will be less food for pollinating insects and, later, less fruit for all. Typically, the loss of one flower equals the loss of one fruit, although for various reasons not all flowers turn into fruit.

This green, common milkweed fruit will eventually dry out and split open, allowing tufted seeds to be dispersed on the wind.

Some fruits don't follow the rules. The fruits of cow parsnip are both dehiscent and indehiscent. They dry and split, but in a way that allows them to retain their seeds.

Unprocessed manoomin requires jigging or threshing.

# Basic Manoomin Preparations

Water is alive.

The recipes in this section are meant to be starting points for your exploration and creativity. They can be altered as you see fit and incorporated and expanded into your own creative dishes. The flour, pudding, and milk are the most exciting in this aspect: go wild; think outside the box. And if you create a winner, I would love to hear all about it.

## Nibi—Water

Before we talk more about manoomin, I'd like to talk about nibi, water. My personal practices with water developed as I searched for ways to heal from past traumas.

I experienced emotional distress flare-ups almost nonstop in my teens and twenties. Surges of stress and anxiety made my body and mind feel as if I was being harmed or was about to be harmed. It was like emotionally reliving the worst things in my life, all the time. It made normal functioning difficult. In my early thirties, after making a huge, more than decade-long effort to change the way I felt and thought—a big portion of that effort having to do with quietly interacting with and observing plants and animals—the repetitive stress was finally less than constant. It was still often enough to make me feel debilitated to an extent. I couldn't control or predict it, other than knowing that it was just going to be there, but by then I knew I was going to get through it.

I was in the shower one evening, emotionally fatigued as usual, and as I let the water run over me I began to notice how it felt when we connected, water to skin. It was as if the water was telling me to listen and focus on what my body was feeling in that moment. This is when I picked up on the space we were both inhabiting, water and me. This is when I began to understand the water was actively with me. That it was conscious and wanted to show me things. To help me. Over the course of five or ten minutes, I don't think I had even one interruption from a stress flare-up. Instead, I was feeling my body in the moment, feeling calmed. Feeling and listening to water. Five or ten minutes of relief might not sound like a lot, but for me it was huge.

I think it was that night that I began leaving half-full glasses of water on the counter any time I would get a drink. I would occasionally bring a glass to sit by my bedside. I would talk to the water. Give thanks. Whisper words of love. And I would feel protected, calmer, loved. Water has helped teach me how to actively feel things in the moment, overriding the stale replaying stress that had held me captive for so long. And ever since, my healing journey has been quite fluid, so to speak.

I share these details so that you understand how I feel about water and what I mean when I say that anytime I'm working with water while I'm cooking, I am thanking it. When I wash my hands or brush my teeth, I talk to the water. Sometimes out loud, sometimes not. But the dialogue is always there. The appreciation is there. The love is there. When you make any of the recipes in this book, I ask that you talk to the water, whatever you want to say. That's how all of the recipes I created for this book were made. Your personal dialogue with water is part of the recipe.

## Notes on Paddy "Wild" Rice

I do not advocate growing and distributing paddy "wild" rice. What we have with paddy rice is a case of stolen identity for profit. Sellers of paddy rice label it as "wild rice," but that's not what it is. The life of true wild rice, manoomin, is not governed by humans and machines. There is something lost when you corral a free spirit into a cage and confine its life to being productive for the sake of profit. There is sadness as well. Many aspects of paddy rice do not vibe with me, and I encourage you to

Wild manoomin has natural variations in color.

Paddy rice is dark and shiny.

## Amikwag (Beavers)

For close to a decade when I was a young woman, I lived by the shore of a very large pond that was more of a small lake, really. In the summertime, I would paddle out in a canoe to watch the ingenuity of amikwag (beavers) in action. They purposefully changed that pond. Their influence was clear. Their handprints were always numerous—fresh indentations along the bottom of channels where they had dug and pressed into the soil.

I saw the development and progression of what I call a floating beaver garden. One summer, a floating mat, about fifty feet in length and thirty feet across, appeared overnight. Over the course of a few summers, I saw how the vegetation on that mat developed in a peculiar way; namely, blue flag irises began to bloom there. I couldn't see them blooming around the border of that pond, just on the mat. After the flowers were present, I would see the beavers dive under the mat through holes in the middle of it and swim underneath and come back up to the surface. They would sit on that mat and eat roots—probably the roots of the blue flags. That is why I call it a floating beaver garden.

The beavers shared their garden with a family of maangwag (common loons), who took shelter from the shoreline predators, making their nest on the floating mat, a sanctuary on which to raise their young. Wazhaskwag (muskrats) would stop on that mat too. I watched those beavers, how they work together to build things, making a better environment for their family. I've had opportunity to eat beaver wiiyaas (meat) over the years, but I think of those beavers and their families, and I just can't bring myself to try it. I know if I was hungry enough I would.

Much can be taught and learned through cooking. For instance, I like to practice mindfulness and channel my intentions in my food preparation and cooking. In preparing soup I thank the nibi, water, with which I wash my hands and vegetables and that I add to the stew to make broth. I give intentional pause to recognize the life stages of the ingredients. The layers of onions and portions of garlic that we eat are modified fleshy leaves. The white part of a leek is sometimes called a psuedostem, as it looks like a stem but is actually a tight grouping of leaf sheaths. Onions, garlic, and leeks are harvested before their flowers have a chance to bloom and produce seeds. Corn and jalapeños, on the other hand, are considered fruit in a botanical sense, meaning the plants they grew on went through all of their earlier stages of life before arriving in my kitchen.

read up on the subject. I don't go around talking bad about paddy rice—I know it's not the rice's fault—but I have gotten upset when it's purchased for community events I've cooked for, especially when I know there are traditional harvesters in those communities.

I don't like stovetop-cooked paddy wild rice. There's little abundance in the way cleaned paddy rice smells coming out of the bag. I would describe the smell as sterile. My senses lack connection to this rice.

I only cook and eat paddy rice when it's been gifted to me, maybe once every couple of years. I don't buy it. I personally prefer to support the traditional ways when it comes to ricing, manoominike, and the people who so lovingly dedicate their energy and spirit to the harvest.

Cooked on the stovetop, paddy rice is chewier and less fluffy than true wild rice, and takes longer to cook. Both true wild rice—manoomin—and paddy wild rice are delicious when toasted, but paddy rice has a texture similar to that of a commercially produced rice cracker, that certain crispness. The toasted seed is sharper and pokes the mouth more than true wild rice, which when toasted has a texture more like a chewy crispness and is fluffier as well. The recipes in this book celebrate the wonder that is true manoomin. Support traditional harvesters and reap the benefits of developing a relationship with this beautifully wild, loving being and food of prophesy.

*Gichi-miigwech to our water protectors: the brave spirits and big hearts who walk a path many cannot. Preserve rice beds: keep oil pipelines out of the waterways.*

Photo by Ivy Vainio

# Cooked Manoomin

VEGAN, GLUTEN FREE                                          Makes 3–4 cups

*There is much debate on the best way to cook a pot of manoomin. Growing up, I heard mostly that you use one part manoomin to two parts nibi (water). This ratio will yield a soft-cooked manoomin if you let it sit until all the water is absorbed. I have always loved soft-cooked manoomin. However, as an adult I find that I enjoy 1:1.75 parts manoomin to nibi even more. This ratio makes for a light, fluffy, and slightly drier result. I personally like the texture in this version a little better and use it in fresh salads and such, where a little more texture to the rice is desirable. For certain grain salads, you might want to use a 1:1.5 ratio.*

1 cup manoomin
1¾ cups nibi (water)

Rinse manoomin in a small pot until the water runs clear, then drain. The rice will remain a little waterlogged. Add 1¾ cups water to pot and bring to a boil; reduce heat to medium, and leave lid slightly offset to allow for a small amount of steam to escape. Cook 25 minutes or until nearly all of the water has been absorbed. Remove from heat and let sit, covered, for 5–10 minutes. Manoomin will absorb any remaining water. Fluff with a fork and serve.

Gently rinse manoomin in cool water until it runs clear.

Perfectly fluffy manoomin that's not too wet is my absolute favorite.

A 1:1.5 manoomin-to-water ratio will give you less curled, denser manoomin, good for grain salads.

## Arne Vainio, MD

Tashia works with Indigenous foods and asked for recipes. I like to cook, and she asked me for my wild rice recipe. At first I was honored she asked me; then I was worried because it's such a simple recipe and I wanted it to be fancier somehow.

I don't necessarily use many ingredients when I cook, and I like to take my time. I've bought some expensive knife sets over the years; once I bought an entire set at a demonstration where the salesman cut through a hammer, then cut a tomato with the same knife. I like my hammers and never had a reason to cut them up. I ended up never using the knives and donated them to a shelter. The knife I use is one my brother found when he was cleaning out a house someone moved from.

I've watched shows with chefs who cut vegetables at high speed and use ingredients I've never even heard of. Suddenly I was aware of those shortcomings. I cut lots of onions and garlic, and it takes me a long time. I don't use processors and machines when I cook and wondered if it was too late to start using them.

When I open the bag and smell the rice, I think back to when I was twelve years old. My grandfather Harry Durant was in boarding school when he was young, and after that he was one of the Ojibwe people who was relocated to Minneapolis to assimilate to help lose the Ojibwe culture. He was beaten in boarding school for speaking Ojibwe and was only taught to work menial jobs, and that's what he did for his entire life. He made ice cream in a state sanitarium and was never promoted beyond that in all his years of service. My grandmother worked in the laundry in the same sanitarium.

My grandfather didn't have anyone to rice with, and he came and picked me up. We didn't have canoe racks like everyone else. He put some old tires on the roof of his car and he took my mother's clothesline and we loaded the canoe on the tires and tied it down. He got mad at me because I slid down in the seat whenever we met another car because I was embarrassed about the old tires on the roof. We got to the rice lake and there were other Ojibwe people he hadn't seen in a long time and he was laughing and joking with them in Ojibwe. I didn't know what they were saying and he didn't introduce me. He took my brother Kelly ricing the year before and they flipped over the canoe when it was full of rice, and that was mostly what I was thinking about.

We paddled to the far end of the lake, and we could hear other people talking and laughing, but they were distant and we only heard them when the wind was right. It was a beautiful sunny day, and ducks and geese were landing and taking off by the thousands. Flocks of red-winged blackbirds would rise in a big black cloud and settle into the rice just as fast. My grandfather had me stand in the front of the canoe. I took the long pole with the fork on the end and he told me how to carefully place it at the base of a clump of rice and slowly push the canoe forward. The bottom of the shallow lake was too soft to just push anywhere. He told me where he wanted me to go, and I slowly pushed us through the rice. I could hear him pulling the rice in with one of the rice knockers and sweeping it into the canoe with the other.

"There are people who beat the rice from the stalks and they get lots of green rice before it's ready. Don't be one of those people. They only do that so they can sell it. You need to leave some for everything else out here."

We riced all day, and other than the sound of an occasional airplane high above, this could have been hundreds of years ago. The sounds of the lake were everywhere, and the geese and ducks were feeding so they could fly south, and I could hear the urgency in their calls.

We didn't flip the canoe and we made it to the landing, where everyone was laughing and joking again. There was a rice buyer there and we sold some of the rice, but the rest we kept to bring to be finished.

Jim Northrup was a good friend of ours, and we used to visit him when he was finishing maple syrup in late winter. We would sit under a shelter and there was a big cast-iron kettle hanging from a tripod. There was a pit dug under the kettle for the base of the fire. Firewood was lined all the way along the kettle, and as it burned away new firewood was put there. The kettle was filled with maple sap and it boiled constantly. The kettle was hanging from a tripod, and there were chairs around the kettle. We sat there and Jim told stories and more stories.

Once in a while the boiling sap would rise and try to overflow the kettle. There was a single piece of bacon hanging from a string over the kettle, and the sap would rise up, touch the bacon and settle back down. "It's the way I was taught," he said.

When I cook wild rice, I think about all of those things. I like cooking and would never call myself a chef. I cook the way my grandmother and my mother cooked. When I cook wild rice, there are many things I feel are important. The first is using real wild rice. I have a friend who used to buy precooked wild rice in cans. I didn't even know that existed. That isn't real wild rice. Neither is the black rice sold in supermarkets or any rice that comes in a box. You need to use real wild rice. If you know which lake it came from, all the better. If you can't harvest it yourself, buy it from someone who does or make sure it's traditionally harvested. We've been buying our rice from Veronica, and she knows the proper ceremonies and the rice we get is clean. Don't offer less when you buy rice from someone who has harvested it. It's a lot of work and the season only lasts a short time and people feed their families with that income. Commercial paddy rice hurts wild rice and should never be used.

*Arne Vainio, MD, is an enrolled member of the Mille Lacs Band of Ojibwe and is a family practice physician on the Fond du Lac reservation in Cloquet, Minnesota. I met Arne a few years back at the American Indian Community Housing Organization in Duluth, at one of their many art and cultural events. I soon became a fan of his work, including his writing. He has an enticing way of telling stories, and I'm honored to include one of his pieces here.*

*Photo by Ivy Vainio*

*Photo by Ivy Vainio*

**Arne Vainio, MD**

# Wild Rice

About half a pound of wild rice. Rinse it well with a strainer. Pour in about a quart of chicken broth. If you don't make your own broth, a thirty-two-ounce container is fine.

About half of a small onion, very finely diced. Some fine-ground black pepper. My uncle Roger covered everything with pepper from one of those square cans. Just a few sprinkles is fine.

Salt. I use Himalayan pink salt from a grinder because it makes me think about how much I use. Someone called me at work once and when I called her back, she talked about Himalayan pink salt for forty-five minutes. I don't remember what she said, but if she liked it that much, it's good enough for me.

Garlic powder. About a teaspoon. If you accidentally put in two teaspoons, that's fine.

A teaspoon of bacon grease. This is the part that made me worry I would lose my credibility as a doctor, but it works to keep the rice from foaming and boiling over as it's cooking, and it's what Jim Northrup would want me to do.

Bring it to a boil, then cover it and turn it down to simmer until all the chicken broth is absorbed or boiled away.

Put a little bit on a small plate or on a small piece of birch bark and put it outside for your ancestors before anyone else eats any. Just a little bit is all that's needed in the spirit world, and the first of it should always go to them.

Share it with someone. This is our ancestral food; this is indigenous food. It's what we need, and it's worth protecting.

# Dry-Toasted Manoomin

VEGAN, GLUTEN FREE

*This method results in a toasted flavor and a dense, not fully popped body. Toasted manoomin can be eaten as is, but it is crunchier than manoomin popped in oil (see page 34). Those with sensitive teeth or who want a softer crunch will want to pop manoomin in oil instead. Toasted manoomin is better for flour making (see page 35); I don't recommend making flour with oil-popped manoomin.*

Heat a pan and drop a few tablespoons up to ¼ cup wild rice seed into the pan at a time. Shake the pan to keep the seeds moving and avoid burning them. When done, manoomin will smell toasted and will have popped open a bit. This should only take seconds if your pan is hot enough. Keep a dish nearby to pour in toasted manoomin to cool while you work on toasting more.

## Puffed Amaranth

To make popped/puffed amaranth, heat a medium pot with a lid over medium-high heat. When the pot is hot, add 1–2 tablespoons of amaranth seed, cover, and shake pot until all of the seeds have popped. This shouldn't take more than a few seconds: just keep shaking! If you add too much seed, you won't get even popping, which can lead to scorching.

Uncooked wild manoomin (left) and toasted wild manoomin (right)

# Oil-Popped Manoomin Two Ways

**VEGAN, GLUTEN FREE**

### Low-Oil Popped Manoomin

Heat a pan, drizzle in 1–2 tablespoons oil, and add enough manoomin to fully coat in the oil (up to ¼ cup). Shake pan until manoomin is popped; it takes only seconds if your pan is hot enough. Remove quickly from heat and cool in a dish lined with paper towels. Season with salt if desired.

### Deep-Oil Popped Manoomin

*This method results in a more-popped, fluffier body. Deep-oil popped manoomin is easier to eat as is; it has less of a hard crunch than toasted manoomin (see page 33), but it doesn't make good flour.*

Pour a couple of inches of oil into a small pot and bring it up to heat (don't let it smoke). Working with small batches and a fine mesh steel strainer, lower manoomin into the oil. If the oil is hot enough, the manoomin will puff up very quickly. Remove from oil and spread manoomin on paper towels to drain. Season with salt if desired.

Whether it's using rice that's at least a year old or making sure you use the hand-parched stuff, everyone who pops their manoomin in deep oil in a saucepan has a trick for what they think contributes to making the best popped manoomin. Some say deep oil is the only way to go and will not bother with any of the other methods. Others prefer not to cook with any oil at all.

# Manoomin Flour

**VEGAN, GLUTEN FREE**　　　　Makes about ¾ cup

*You can use raw or toasted manoomin for flour. I prefer raw when using flour in baked goods and toasted for recipes like Ginger Maple Sugar Manoomin Dust (page 122) that can benefit from a toasted flavor. In other words, use toasted flour if you're not going to further cook the flour in a recipe.*

**1 cup manoomin**

I like to make small batches of manoomin flour, placing between ½ cup and no more than 1 cup of manoomin in a powerful blender and blending until very fine and smooth. The more you add, the longer each batch will take. You will need to stop and scrape or tap down the sides about every 30 seconds or so. You will know you're getting close to having the right consistency when very fine manoomin dust streams into the air as you open the lid. Flour should be very fine and silky feeling when rubbed between your fingers. It takes me about 3 minutes of solid blending to make one small batch.

Use a strong blender and keep a dish nearby to pour your flour into.

Manoomin flour should be fine and silky.

# Manoomin for Milk and Pudding

VEGAN, GLUTEN FREE                                                    Makes 4 cups

*Use this basic manoomin recipe, which yields just the right consistency to blend smoothly, for pudding and milk for making pies, cookies, and other baked goods. This recipe produces enough manoomin for one batch of Manoomin Milk (page 37) and one batch of Basic Manoomin Pudding (page 38), both of which will give you enough for two of any of the manoomin pie recipes in this book that call for pudding.*

**1 cup manoomin**
**3 cups nibi (water)**

In a large pot, combine manoomin and water. Bring to a boil, then reduce heat and simmer for 20 minutes with cover slightly askew to allow a little steam to escape. Remove from heat, cover, and let sit 10 minutes.

Use 1 cup of this cooked manoomin for Manoomin Milk (page 37) and remaining 3 cups cooked manoomin for Basic Manoomin Pudding (page 38).

# Manoomin Milk

VEGAN, GLUTEN FREE                    Makes 2¾ cups

*Manoomin milk works well on granola cereal and oatmeal and in many recipes that call for milk. Leave out the sugar, salt, and vanilla for a plain milk. This ratio yields milk of a thickness similar to store-bought almond milk.*

1 cup hot Manoomin for Milk and
    Pudding (page 36; see tip)
2½ cups nibi (water)
1 tablespoon maple sugar
½ teaspoon vanilla extract
pinch salt

Put all ingredients in a food processor or blender and blend for about 5 minutes, stopping to scrape the sides as needed, until milk is super smooth. Add more water for thinner milk. Cool and serve. Store in an airtight jar or bottle in the refrigerator and shake well before using. Use within a few days.

> **TIP:** Hot manoomin—especially overcooked hot manoomin that is nice and wet and squishy—makes for a smoother milk.

One batch of manoomin milk makes about 2¾ cups.

# Basic Manoomin Pudding

VEGAN, GLUTEN FREE                                        Makes 2–3 cups

3 cups hot Manoomin for Milk and Pudding (page 36)
⅓ cup + 3 tablespoons hot Manoomin Milk (page 37)

Combine hot cooked manoomin and milk in a strong blender and blend until
smooth, scraping sides as needed. It will take a little time to get to the right
consistency—like smooth, thick oatmeal. It should hold its shape if you wiggle it
on a spoon. Let pudding cool before using in pie recipes. Store in the refrigerator.
Use within a few days.

# Manoomin Maple Seed Mix

VEGAN, GLUTEN FREE     Makes 4 cups

*Leaving some larger pieces will yield a more visually appealing mix when used for a crust, granola, or Love Bites (page 174). Or, if you want less chew in your crust, powder the mix as fine as you wish.*

1 cup raw, shelled pumpkin seeds
1 cup raw, shelled sunflower seeds
1 cup Popped Manoomin (page 34)
1 cup Puffed Amaranth (page 33)
½ teaspoon salt
½ cup maple sugar

Use a food processor or blender to break up pumpkin seeds, sunflower seeds, and manoomin into small pieces (see tip). Pour into a large bowl and stir in amaranth and salt. Use a blender to whirl maple sugar until smooth, then add to the rest of the ingredients. Mix well.

> **TIP:** To avoid making too fine a powder when using a blender, pause after a few pulses to push the top unchopped seeds down and/or work in small batches.

Manoomin Maple Seed Mix

# Manoomin Pie Crust

VEGAN, GLUTEN FREE                                      Makes 2 (9-inch) pie shells

*This crust can be used in recipes that call for baked, prebaked, and no-bake crusts. Dough can be stored for a few days in the fridge in a tightly sealed container.*

1 batch Manoomin Maple Seed Mix (page 39)
up to ½ cup nibi (water)

If the pie recipe calls for a prebaked crust, heat oven to 350 degrees. Grease pie pans.

Put Manoomin Maple Seed Mix in a large bowl and add water a little at a time, stirring well after each addition, until the mixture is shapeable. You will be surprised how much difference a little water makes if you keep stirring. For a no-bake crust, add very little water (less water equals more crumb). In any case, don't add more than ½ cup water total, less for a no-bake recipe.

Press dough into prepared pans. It will be sticky and delicious. Good luck not eating all of it straight from the bowl!

For a raw, no-bake crust, stop here, cover, and put into the fridge to harden. Always keep your crust covered.

For a baked pie, fill crust and continue as instructed. As the pie cools, the crust will crisp. For a soft and crumbly crust, cover for a while as pie cools before serving.

For a prebaked crust, bake 16 minutes or until edges start to brown. The middle and sides will feel soft. Let crust almost cool, then use with any no-bake pie recipe. If you cover the pie for a while before serving, the crust will be soft and crumbly, similar to a graham cracker crust. Leave pie uncovered for a crisp crust.

Prebaked manoomin pie crust

## Intentional Reimaginings:
## We're All in This Together

On a wintry night in 2019, after praying in bed for an hour or more, I began to toss and turn, my entire body pulsating with anxiety and concernedness. I had the future of manoomin, Aki (Earth), and the Anishinaabeg on my mind.

It was then that manoominikaa (much wild rice) appeared around my bed, encircling me with a fullness to their form, bringing water and wind and even sunlight shining through, kissing their dancing form to radiate into my awareness. They came with this wider sense of identity; they came as the place where they grow and have roots, the place they love and call home—their direct lifeline. The plants surrounded me, to comfort me and to be known in this way.

And then the manoomin spoke: "We're going to be alright, we're going to be alright, we're going to be alright." Over and over they assured me, and my tenseness began to release, and as they spoke to me about the future of their well-being, I began to feel the future of my own well-being assured. I know that I am much more than a physical form. My identity and well-being are tied to the manoomin and the environment, and our well-being is one and the same.

In the wake of a global pandemic, the Black Lives Matter movement's call for justice, and impending environmental disasters related to climate change, it is more important than ever to reimagine and commit to changing our way of interacting with one another and our Maamaa Aki, Mother Earth. We must be intentional with how we share spaces, how we eat, how we gather our food, how we know and relate empathetically to each other and those beings who provide us with sustenance. Healthy communities foster healthy emotional sustenance, and healthy food helps build healthy bodies. Sometimes a little imagination can go a long way toward setting ourselves back down on that good path. It will take all of our reimaginings combined moving forward. We all have a part in bringing in new ways of being together. I've come to know that most of my reimaginings revolve around what I know best: food and the environment.

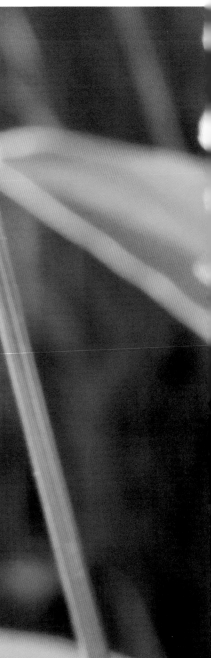

# Ziigwang
## (ZEE gwuhng)

# SPRING

Looking into the seasons as they arise, we look forward while looking back. Woods huddle in their brown, early-spring, leaf-litter blankets. Dancing in the potential of that space, an abundance of green shakes, unfurling into timeless, starlight-filled air. For now, they dance in the womb of this place, but we know they're there.

For the Anishinaabeg, iskigamizigan (sugar bush) marks the start of a new year. Often it is a family and community affair. More hands means more wood chopped and hauled, more sap collected, fires tended, and bubbling kettles watched.

## Akawe Gidasemaakemin— First We Offer Tobacco

There's no satisfaction like locating, harvesting, preparing, sharing, and eating wild foods. Whether stopping to smell and eat the flowers or fruits while out hiking or taking fiddleheads and other wild herbaceous foods home to cook, store, and/or share, embodying a connection to the source makes the whole process enjoyable. The emotional sustenance gifted us by harvesting and processing wild food flows through the brain to trigger all the right places. Happiness is generated and thrives in the movement of the journey of nourishing our bodies through the seasons.

Akawe gidasemaakemin—first, we offer tobacco.

Asemaa refers to the inner bark and/or leaves of a variety of plants that are offered during prayer and at other times, such as when we ask an elder or knowledge keeper for help or guidance (this includes when we ask our plant elders for help, too). Asemaa can be the inner bark of the red dogwood, or red willow, which

Juicy maple tree flower buds: a good sign of spring

 Herbaceous wild foods are the tender parts of annual or perennial plants that die back after each reproductive season and grow anew the next year. They include graminoids like manoomin (although it's the seeds of the manoomin plant that are eaten), forbs such as common milkweed, curly dock (which is a delicious invasive species), and ferns.

Collecting sap.
*Photo by Jason Hart*

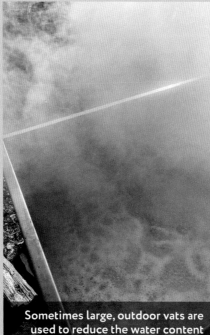

Sometimes large, outdoor vats are used to reduce the water content of maple sap. *Photo by Jason Hart*

Zhiiwaagamizigan, maple syrup. *Photo by Jason Hart*

Sap is further reduced indoors on the stovetop. *Photo by Jason Hart*

## Ziinzibaakwadwaaboo— Maple Sap

Maple sap is collected in late winter/early spring before the trees' flowers burst open and the frogs start to sing. People use buckets, bags, and other containers to gather the sap to be boiled in big vats or kettles. Often it is reduced even further on the stovetop in the kitchen.

## Ziinzibaakwad—Maple Sugar

Maple sugar is made from maple syrup, which contains minerals, trace elements, and the antioxidant quebecol, which studies have shown to kill certain types of cancer cells and which has only ever been found in pure maple syrup products. Maple sugar is a natural mood elevator and an easy-to-carry source of antioxidants and calories. The sugaring process is a good activity for the whole family. Maple sap is collected in the springtime and boiled down, concentrating into maple syrup, which is used to make maple sugar. Tapping trees, hanging sap buckets, collecting and carrying sap, tending the fire, taking turns watching the sap boil, and later agitating syrup to make sugar and sugar cakes is both work and fun—and something more easily managed when done as a family or community.

TIP: Blending maple sugar in a blender creates powdered maple sugar.

Ziinzibaakwad, maple sugar, is softer to the touch than granulated sugar, has a flavor similar to light brown sugar but milder, and has an almost creamy taste.

Miskwaabiimag (aka red willow, aka dogwood)

is gathered in the spring when the outer bark is bright red. It can also be *Nicotiana rustica*, *Nicotiana tabacum*, as well as an individual's personal selection of plants or plant blends for this purpose. Blends are also sometimes called kinnikinnick.

There is the offering of asemaa (traditional "tobacco") or tobacco. There is prayer. And there are conversations held with plants. At the start of relationships with most plants I have interacted with, the conversations, when initiated, are very short, like first introductions often are. Having a plant introduce itself is similar to the experience of sensing the emotional state of another person. You can feel them. My interactions with plants have evolved over years. Some years I make no movement to gather certain plants; I simply observe and listen, feel, sense.

My advice is to practice being a good listener. Over the years of getting to know different plants, I've been directed to where plants are growing and told how many leaves to pick down to the exact number, which patches of plants are better to pick in, and which plants to let alone—all from the plants themselves. You will come across plants that are in poor health. Be kind and say a prayer for them or give them words of love. There is nothing impossible about talking to plants if one practices good listening. To have conversations, you also must talk. Talk to the plants and they will tell you many things. Just know that they can tell you things in different ways, whether through feelings, images, the transference of knowing, or words. The words will sound different than words entering your physical ears. Be on alert for any form of communication, and you will be on your way to having your own conversations with plants. The same holds true for animals as well.

One plant has repeatedly called for my attention spring after spring. One year, I felt drawn to actually eat a portion of the shoot of this plant. It didn't take very long for my heart to start racing. I didn't eat but a small bite. After that—it's been years since—I have not eaten this plant again. I have not been given any reason to. I have not been told what this plant can be used for medicinally, other than knowing it affects the heart and blood. I do know it is not a plant to be eaten in any great amount. I am still called by this plant every year. Maybe one year, I will learn more. The lesson here is that building real relationships with plants takes a lifetime; be patient and enjoy the journey.

When it comes to manoomin, I do not advocate that everyone eat manoomin, nor do I insist they rush out to find some in the wild. I do advocate that if you are from an Anishinaabe community where harvesters live and want to learn how to harvest, give a harvester some asemaa and ask for help. I can only give advice about the foodways and protocols I know. I do not claim to know much, but I do know that you have to give respect to get it. If you are not Anishinaabe but would like to learn more, I suggest seeking out harvesters in your local community and asking if they're comfortable sharing about manoomin with you. If yes, great; if not, don't take it personally. Keep moving forward, building those relationships. The learning will come.

## Common Wild Spring Foods of Minnesota
### Zesegaandagoog, Gaawaandagoog— Black Spruces, White Spruces

Spruce and pine needles are, in a botanical sense, modified leaves. They are green because they have chlorophyll and make sugars the plant needs, just like those of species with more recognizable "leaf" structures. I love munching a few spruce tips raw and blending them fresh with oils and seasonings and salt for a bright pop of citrus-like flavor. They also dehydrate and store well

Spruce tips when young are very tender.

# Gaandakii'iganaakoon—Ricing Push Poles

**JUNE 7, 2019**

**SOUTH BOUNDARY ROAD, RED LAKE RESERVATION**

I follow my dad, crouching down to walk under spruce boughs, crunching dried needles underfoot, the smell of sap thick in the air. "Here's one," he says, looking up a tall balsam sapling.

"See how much smaller that is?" He's referring to the ones we'd looked at earlier that were about four inches in diameter. "And I can use almost the whole thing, all the way down to here, 'cause it's not that big," He reaches down to grab the base about three inches above the ground, using the size of his fist to compare to the tree's girth, which is a little smaller.

"And then we're still going to lose about an eighth of an inch width after we get all of the bark off. That's nice and straight; I like this one. And I can use it all the way up there"—he swats a mosquito off his face without skipping a beat—"about fifteen, sixteen feet, maybe, which is about a typical size for a pole. And we won't have to take much off the end when we're done, to get it to fit inside the duckbill."

Dad goes back to his truck to get his asemaa, and after he's put it down by the base of the tree he uses the flat back of his maul to remove all of the lowest branches so he can go to work bringing the tree down. While he's working he stops to tell me, "And this one's a balsam, it's got the flat needles. It's not a spruce, but it's nice and straight." He makes short work of bringing it down.

After we haul it back out to the road, he walks the length of it, measuring it with his feet. About fourteen feet.

We take the rest of the branches off and, after getting sap on him, I tease him that he's a sappy pappy.

Over the course of an hour or so, we find a total of three good saplings for ricing poles, all of which he ties to the top of his pickup truck.

On the ride back to his house, he tells me, "One year, your grandpa had me make poles for that camp wilderness. I musta made six to seven poles that year. I made 'em all long. And they went up to the Northwest Angle, and all them guys needed poles. They had canoes but no poles. And I let 'em borrow all my poles, and pretty soon they said they were too heavy and too long, and they ended up cutting five to six feet off each pole just to make 'em lighter. They made a whole pack, a buncha little short poles," he chuckles. "Those poles were still wet when they used them, only dried out about two weeks, maybe. So they were heavier."

"I rub my hand down them as I work, to make sure they're smooth so you barely need to go over them with sandpaper. Then you'll go just barely, over the knots," he tells me after we've gotten the poles back to his house out on Highway 89, a few miles south of the village of Red Lake. By this point, he has peeled off the bark and is running his knife over the pokey remnants of branches.

He carves down the thick end, where the tree had been closest to the ground. "The first time I went ricing, back in, musta been 1975, we had to drag the canoes out in the woods for about a mile one way, then rice all day, and drag everything all the way back. Me and my cousin went together. We watched the ducks eating rice, and were just having a blast, out there on the water. We thought we got a lot of rice. When we got it back and weighed it, it was twelve pounds." He laughs. "So that was my first ricing experience. And it was just down the road five miles, at a lake called Fallhall Lake."

We check to see if the end is close to the size needed to fit into the duckbill, also called a marsh foot, the piece that helps you push yourself along better in the canoe. "I'll leave this part just a little bigger than the end of the duckbill, so it compresses when we put it on and it's not loose." There are different kinds of duckbills. Some people even make them out of wood, like the ricers in Fond du Lac; I've seen their poles with the wood ones on them. He taps gently on the middle part of the duckbill with the back of his hatchet, wedging it onto the pole. It fits nice and snug. "When the water soaks in, it will swell and tighten up if it happens to be a little loose here and there."

We stand the poles up and lean them on a tree to get them off the ground to dry for a couple of months before ricing season starts. "They'll be lighter then," he says looking up at them. Their size reminds him of a story.

"Before, I used to make poles that were so long they thought Naanabozho was coming through the rice bed, 'cause they could see my pole waaaaay up in the air. I don't know how many times they'd say, 'Hey! We thought Naanabozho was coming through here!'" He laughs.

He rotates one that has a very slight wave on the thinner end of it. "We'll let it sit like this for a while; the weight of the pole will help correct that dip. It won't be perfect, but it will straighten out a bit."

I heard someone ask my dad to compare the modern aluminum pole with a wood pole. His reply: "That's one thing I can't compare, because I've never used one. I've seen them used on the lakes before, you know, but I never did. It didn't seem right to me. I always enjoyed making my own things."

if kept out of the sunlight. Dehydrated tips make a lovely tea. Spruce needles are high in vitamin C. The pitch of the tree makes canoes watertight, and the rootlets make great lashing. Instead of utilizing flowers to produce their seeds, spruce grow and protect their seeds in cones. Thus, they are conifers. They like to inhabit bogs and are often found with tamarack trees.

### Waagaagan—Fiddleheads

Ferns in their young, unfurling, "fiddlehead" stage are an exquisite treat when steamed or sauteed. I have only worked with the ostrich fern (*Matteuccia struthiopteris*),

Ferns and leeks can often be found growing together.

The fiddlehead-shaped shoots of ostrich fern emerge as juicy green coils.

but many folks tell me of other fern species they eat, depending on their location. Most if not all fiddleheads should be cooked prior to eating. Fiddleheads have an abundance of antioxidants, omega fatty acids, and vitamins A and C. They also have fiber as well as minerals like iron, calcium, and potassium. Both the taste and the texture are similar to asparagus with a bit of green bean and cucumber mixed in.

### Zhigaagawanzhiig—Wild Leeks

Wild leeks (aka ramps) like to grow with ostrich fern, and often they are ready for harvest at the same time. Finding a healthy community of these two plants growing together makes for a heavenly good day. Because they

Fresh wild ramp leaves with dried flowers and fruit from last season still inside

Basal leaves of wild leek

## PLANT DIARY, MARCH 10, 2021

The crows have been making their presence known this last week here along the shore of Gichigami, building a nest at the top of the big pine on the edge of the lakeshore. I wonder about the eagle family living next door, and their young one who must have left the nest by now. We'd seen it flying up and down the shore the last couple of months, as big as its parents, still mottled in color and with no distinct white head plumage yet. I haven't seen them in weeks. I will put out some asemaa and wish their family well for the new year. It feels like a great time to be making prayers for the health and well-being of all.

I've been wondering about the large maple in the backyard. With word of sugar bush going on all across Minnesota the last week or so, I can't help but look at its glorious, wide-spreading form. But I will not tap it. I will wait until next year; hopefully I will have more time then to make a sugar bush camp.

Gichigami

reproduce very slowly—their life cycle can take up to ten years—you should never pull up their bulbs, or even a good portion of them. I mostly harvest the tender, green leaves. I harvest the bulbs only when I find a large and very dense patch, and then I pull up just a few here and there where they look most crowded. They are a delicious addition to just about any savory dish and have flavonoids, vitamins, minerals, and fiber. I like to dehydrate the leaves and munch on a few plain as a tasty snack.

### Doodooshaaboojiibikan—Dandelions, "Milk Root"

Dandelions restore energy and vitality after the hardships of winter. They can help detoxify the blood and liver and are full of vitamins and minerals. Young leaves and flowers are eaten fresh. Older leaves are cooked to reduce bitterness. Roots can be scrubbed, roasted, and steeped in water like tea. Dandelion is also sometimes used in poultice form to treat skin ailments. As a child, I learned that splitting the stems of dandelions with my thumbnail revealed juicy interiors that provide a soothing relief for the itch and mild pain of mosquito bites.

### Ode'iminan—Strawberries, "Heart Berry"

Strawberries are high in flavonoids and phytonutrients, which contribute to heart health. They are a natural mood elevator, and an excellent source of vitamin C.

Tiny strawberries hide under compound, trifoliate leaves (each leaf has three leaflets).

Strawberries have "perfect" flowers.

After the little white flowers of the strawberry plant have fallen, sweet red fruits grow, peeking out from under the plant's three leaflets in late spring to early summer. Strawberries usually ripen a couple of months after maple sugar camp is over and before the blueberries are ripe. Some years and in some regions, certain patches ripen around the same time as the blueberries. Strawberries are delicious in salads, mixed-berry jams and fruit leather, and granola-berry blends. Dried strawberries are also a great addition to wild tea blends.

## Mints

Sunny Minnesota fields are great places to find an abundance of mint plants of various species. Two of my favorites to harvest are wild bergamot and hyssop—and luckily they're often found growing side by side. Wild bergamot has a flavor very much like the bergamot of Earl Grey tea. In late spring to early summer, I harvest the "peppery" young shoots and leaves. In the summer,

I harvest the bright purple flowers that remind me of bursting fireworks. Wild bergamot has many names in different languages. Some know it as a love medicine; others for how it helps with digestion. I've been told it has the ability to help heal bones as well. No doubt there are many other benefits to forming a relationship with this plant.

Another common mint is the hyssop, also known by a variety of names. The flavor of its leaves and flowers is of anise. Naturally sweet tasting, like wild bergamot it is a great addition to tea blends, jams, sauces, and other recipes where tea is used to add extra flavor and dimension. Mints are pretty easy to spot, as most of them have square stems, an uncommon characteristic. These mints are herbs/forbs, have opposite leaves, and are monoecious.

Bergamot and hyssop grow side by side.

Wild bergamot

## Apakweshkwayag—Cattails

In the spring and early summer, young, tender cattail shoots can be harvested and eaten raw or cooked. Enlist the help of a teacher as you learn to identify cattails in their young shoot stage, as there are look-alikes. I've been told that in early summer, the green, immature flower spikes can be steamed and eaten, although I've never tried them myself. After the flowers develop further, some people collect pollen from them and add it to flour for baking. Cattails contain fiber, vitamins, and minerals. They are caretakers and defenders of the water, taking up pollutants from where they grow. You don't want to ingest these pollutants, however, so harvest cattails from clean water. Cattail leaf mats have long been used to insulate wiigiwaaman (lodges), and the dry fluff of the cattail heads is used as a natural absorbing material in diapers and as stuffing and insulation for toys, pillows, blankets, and more.

Cattail

## Miziseg—Turkeys

Based on their abundant presence along roadsides in the spring and fall, turkeys seem ubiquitous in the northland, but they were eradicated in Minnesota about a century ago due to the rapid destruction of habitats and overhunting. Efforts to bring them back were successful, and I'm happy every time I see them in the wild. Turkeys are hardy birds. They don't migrate. They stick out the cold winters and piling snow like the rest of us northerners. Turkeys nest on the ground in the springtime, and in the winter they roost in conifers and other trees offering protection from blizzards and freezing temperatures.

On occasion I will eat turkey meat. When I do, I always think about the history of the turkey's journey—from wild turkeys being exterminated in our state to now having the most domestic turkeys in the country right here; from living free to living on farms; from populating the forests to populating the frozen section at grocery stores. I try to get turkey meat from free-range farms. It's good to think about the animal's life as just that—a life.

### MARCH 13, 2021

The young eagle paid me a visit this morning. As I was typing some of the last pieces for *The Good Berry Cookbook* at my dining room table, I looked out the window to see it coming at our home from the south. It looked in on me before circling back around over the house, going off on fine eagle business, no doubt. I got a sense that the young eagle is going to be just fine. This in turn made me feel like I, too, will be just fine.

# Manoomin Wraps

**VEGETARIAN, GLUTEN FREE**                    Makes 4 (6-inch) wraps

*Serve these wraps stuffed with a hash of chopped venison, wild leek, and scrambled eggs—so tasty, you might want to double the wrap recipe to have seconds. These are also delicious wrapped around Sweet Potato Corn Pudding with Rose Sauce (page 154) and fresh diced fruit. Or serve with Avocado Salad (page 104) and crushed corn tortilla chips.*

⅓ cup Manoomin Flour (page 35)          2 eggs
⅓ cup milk (almond or other)            ¼ teaspoon salt

In a bowl, mix flour, milk, eggs, and salt by hand, then transfer to a blender and blend until light and fluffy, 20–30 seconds. If the mixture is not well blended, with air incorporated, the wraps will be lumpy and not have the right texture.

Heat a nonstick skillet over medium heat (see tip). Working with ¼ cup batter at a time, pour in the batter while swirling the pan, making the wraps as large and thin as possible—about 6 inches wide. After about 30 seconds, the sides will pull up off the pan and the bubbles will dry out. Flip and cook for another 30 seconds. Remove from pan to a plate and cover with a lid to keep warm and moist until it's time to eat.

Leftover wraps can be loosely rolled and stored in an airtight container in the refrigerator for a few days. Before filling, gently warm in a skillet or pop in the microwave for a few seconds, keeping them covered to maintain flexibility.

> **TIP:** If the heat is too high, you won't be able to swirl the batter thin enough. Thicker wraps are more likely to crack when you wrap them around your breakfast scramble of choice.

Diana and her daughter harvesting birch bark.
*Image courtesy Diana Bird*

*Diana Bird has a degree in psychology from the University of Saskatchewan and a degree in Indigenous social work from the First Nations University of Canada. She is a mother, the coauthor of* From the Birds: A Family Cook Book, *and a fellow member of the I-Collective. Diana lives in Saskatchewan, where she is on the board of directors at Montreal Lake Cree Nation Urban Services Inc. and works as a student retention specialist at First Nations University of Canada. She does such great work in her community, and I am oh so happy to be able to share her tasty recipe for Wild Rice Cakes with you all.*

### Diana Bird
# Wild Rice Cakes

GLUTEN FREE                                          Serves 8

*Serve these rice cakes with butternut squash soup made with curry and coconut milk.*

| | |
|---|---|
| 4 cups cooked wild rice | 1 egg |
| 1 onion, shredded | salt and pepper to taste |
| 2 cloves garlic, minced | 2 teaspoons bacon fat |

Mix together wild rice, onion, garlic, egg, and salt and pepper.

In a saucepan, put down 4 round cookie cutters (see tip). Add bacon fat and heat, then add a couple teaspoons of the wild rice mixture to each cookie cutter and fry until browned and crispy. Flip over and cook the other side.

TIP: Use canning jar lid rings for holding the cake shape.

Wild Rice Cakes served with soup.
*Image courtesy Diana Bird*

# Nutty Manoomin Patties

VEGAN, GLUTEN FREE                    Makes about 20–25 (3-ounce) patties

*This recipe was developed for an episode of* Family Ingredients *featuring the story of Valerie Kaneshiro. Valerie grew up on the Lac Courte Oreilles reservation in Wisconsin until moving to the island of Kaua'i, where she and her family raised award-winning hogs. In the episode, she travels back to her hometown in search of a food memory: waagaagan—fiddleheads. My heart was heavy when I heard Valerie had passed away in the fall of 2020. She is loved and remembered by many. To learn about Valerie's touching story, watch* Family Ingredients, *season 2, episode 3.*

2 cups manoomin
Manoomin Flour (page 35) as needed
1–2 cups diced and roasted
    mixed mushrooms, leeks,
    or onions, optional

salt
1 cup Puffed Amaranth (page 33)
shelled, crushed, and roasted
    wild hazelnuts
sunflower oil for frying

Cook manoomin in 5 cups of water until the rice pops open and begins to curl. Remove half of the rice and set aside. Continue cooking the other half until very soft, about 10 more minutes, adding more water as needed. Drain rice and, while still hot, blend in a food processor until smooth. Remove to a bowl and add flour a little at a time until the mixture can hold the shape of a patty. Add some of the reserved wild rice and mushrooms, leeks, and/or onions (if using)—as much as you like, as long as the mixture is still easily shapeable. Season mixture with salt to taste.

In a shallow dish, stir together amaranth and hazelnuts. Form manoomin mixture into half-inch-thick patties about 2½ inches in diameter, and gently press both sides into amaranth-hazelnut mixture. Fry in a small amount of sunflower oil until each side is golden brown and crisp but insides are still soft.

# Nutty Manoomin Patties with Hominy and Wild Greens

**VEGAN, GLUTEN FREE**                                                      Serves 2

*Two foods I love in combination are hominy and manoomin. This dish is an ode to the happy "music" I've always felt when eating them—the kind of music that makes you dance in your seat as you eat.*

1 tablespoon oil or butter
½ cup chopped mushrooms
¼ cup chopped wild leek or
    1 tablespoon minced garlic
1 cup broth

1½ cups cooked hominy
1 cup chopped fresh wild greens
    of your choice—mix it up!
salt to taste
Nutty Manoomin Patties (page 62)

Heat oil or butter in a skillet over medium heat and add the mushrooms. Cook for about 2–3 minutes, stirring as mushrooms soften. Add leeks or garlic and broth. Cover and cook another 2–3 minutes. Add hominy, wild greens, and salt. Cook, covered, stirring occasionally, until hominy is soft and hot. Uncover and let liquid reduce a bit if desired. Spoon over Nutty Manoomin Patties and serve hot.

Harvested leek leaves

# Nutty Manoomin Patties with Squash and Fiddlehead-Nettle Puree

VEGAN, GLUTEN FREE                                                    Serves 4–5

*The puree in this recipe is similar to a kale pesto my friend and colleague Vern DeFoe developed for the Tatanka Truck menu. I liked that he would use pumpkin seeds and sumac, and I adapted his recipe to incorporate wild greens. I hope you love the savory, nutty, and wild flavors in this dish as much as I do.*

1 butternut squash
½ cup condensed tea (see tip); I
    used wild swamp tea, mukigobug
    aniibiish, aka Labrador tea or
    ledum tea (see page 185)
1 cup shelled pumpkin seeds
1 tablespoon salt
1 tablespoon powdered sumac

1 cup sunflower oil
2 cups blanched fiddlehead ferns
2 cups blanched stinging nettles
Nutty Manoomin Patties (page 62)
Puffed Amaranth (page 33), optional
wild garnishes like apple
    blossoms, immature spruce
    cones, wild mint, optional

Heat oven to 350–375 degrees. Cut squash in half lengthwise and remove seeds with a spoon (see tip). Rub the squash with a little sunflower oil and put face down on a parchment paper–lined baking pan. Roast until squash is soft, about 30–35 minutes. Cool. Scoop the creamy squash out of the skin and into a food processor. Blend with tea to a scoopable but not runny consistency. Set aside.

In a food processor, blend pumpkin seeds, salt, sumac, sunflower oil, fiddlehead ferns, and stinging nettles until smooth but not runny, adding more oil and salt as needed.

Top Nutty Manoomin Patties with the tea-infused squash, the fiddlehead-nettle puree, a sprinkle of puffed amaranth, and any of your favorite wild garnishes like apple blossoms, immature spruce cones, or wild mint.

> **TIPS:** To make condensed tea, place tea in pot with less water than your recipe calls for and let simmer on low until it is darker in color and stronger in flavor than a normal batch for sipping.
>
> Wash, dry, and store squash seeds for planting as desired.

Dried sumac

Beautiful butternut squash, spaghetti squash, and pumpkin. There are lots of squashes to try!

# Manoomin Breakfast Pies

**VEGETARIAN, GLUTEN FREE**

Follow the recipe for Nutty Manoomin Patties (page 62), but instead of making patties press mixture by hand into 6-inch shells, as thin as dough allows. If batter is too sticky, add a little more flour.

Fill each shell with scrambled eggs, cooked beans, wild greens, roasted mushrooms, a sprinkle of salt—whatever you want. Gently fold over one side and press edges together with a fork. Press pies into the amaranth-hazelnut mixture.

Heat a skillet over medium heat, add 1–2 tablespoons oil, and fry a couple pies at a time, flipping to brown each side. Top with salsa if desired.

**Photo by Nedahness Greene**

*Deanna StandingCloud is a citizen of the Red Lake Nation of Anishinaabe. She is a mother, playwright, organizer, community leader, powwow emcee, and student of the Ojibwe language. She works for the Aanjibimaadizing Program with the Mille Lacs Band of Ojibwe. Deanna enjoys spending time with her beautiful children, Breanna, Kylie, Nigozis, and Ziigwan. They enjoy attending traditional ceremonies, taking nature walks, creating art, and cooking yummy food. I am inspired by everything Deanna does, and I love how nutritious this recipe is and how good eating a bowl of this porridge makes you feel.*

**Deanna StandingCloud**

# Quinoa and Wild Rice Porridge

VEGAN, GLUTEN FREE                              Serves 6

*This hearty breakfast will keep you feeling full all morning!*

1 cup wild rice, rinsed and drained
ground cinnamon
ground nutmeg
vanilla extract
1 cup quinoa, rinsed and drained

2 tablespoons pure maple syrup or honey
1½ cups milk (almond or rice milk)
¾ cup seasonal berries (or dried cranberries or fruit)
½ cup chopped walnuts

Place wild rice in a deep saucepan and add water to cover by about an inch (about 2 cups water). Add ½ teaspoon cinnamon and ½ teaspoon nutmeg, then bring to a boil. Cover and simmer for 20–25 minutes; stir in 1 teaspoon vanilla just at the end.

In a separate pan, add quinoa with 2 cups water and a dash of cinnamon and nutmeg. Bring to a boil; reduce heat, cover, and simmer for 15 minutes, until quinoa becomes opaque. Just before it has completely absorbed all the water, stir in a splash of vanilla.

In a large bowl, mix together quinoa, wild rice, maple syrup or honey, and milk. Serve warm in bowls and top with berries and walnuts.

**Image courtesy Marsha Reeves**

*Maadho'okiid Marsha Traxler Reeves is of Mohawk and Ojibwe descent, Turtle Clan of the Haudenosaunee. She is a grandmother, holistic nurse, swamp singer, women's traditional dancer, Anishinaabemowin student, and gatherer of traditional Indigenous foods and medicines. She lives in an award-winning energy-efficient, solar-powered house in the woods near the Muskegon River in Michigan. Water address: first bayou on your right as you float downstream from Croton Dam.*

*I know Marsha from community art and cultural events we both attend in the Duluth area. Running into her is always a joy: she has lots of knowledge and loves to share. Marsha's recipe is full of life and flavor and demonstrates the restorative nature of wiisiniwin (food).*

*Maadho'okiid Marsha Traxler Reeves, Mohawk and Ojibwe, holistic nurse*

# Manoomin and Mushrooms

GLUTEN FREE                                                    Serves 3

*Maybe you have venison bones in your freezer that you've been waiting to make stock with. Spring is a great time to utilize homemade stocks and get a vitality boost. For the mushrooms, any kind will do, and it's fun to experiment. You can also add ramps, either raw greens or chopped bulb, to the rice before cooking, or add dried ramps with the mushrooms.*

3 cups venison bone broth (see below)
1 cup wild lake rice
1 cup chopped wild mushrooms

In a large pot, combine broth and rice, bring to a boil, and remove from heat. Add mushrooms, stir well, and cover. Let sit for 20 minutes, then peek to see if rice has absorbed all the broth. If so, it's ready to serve. If not, bring to a boil again and simmer gently until broth is absorbed, about 2–3 minutes, depending on the rice variety.

# Venison Bone Broth

Fill pressure cooker with venison bones; some meat on them is okay. Add water to cover bones, 1–2 tablespoons salt, and ¼ cup vinegar. Cook under pressure 2 hours. Cool, then separate bones and meat and broth.

Alternatively, put the bones in a slow cooker, cover with water, and simmer for 4–8 hours.

If you don't have venison bones, shave small pieces of (untreated) antler into boiling water and let it simmer for a while. I use about a thumb-size piece shaved into 1 gallon of water. This tip is from Daisy Kostus. Thank you, Daisy!

In any way you use water for cooking, use broth to add precious minerals to your meal.

Shaggy mane mushrooms are one of the edible species in the Midwest. This batch was harvested for the Red Lake Nation Food Summit a few years back. To learn more about wild mushrooms, seek out a mushroom guide.

# Bison and Sunroot Quick Stew

GLUTEN FREE                                                                                    Serves 3

*Bison and sunroots are indigenous to North America. As new flower stalks grow, giizisoojiibikag (sunroots) represent the earth and grounding, life and rebirth. Cooking bison and sunroots together is like a recipe or prayer for the resurgence of mashkode-bizhikiwag (bison) upon Gimaamaanaan Aki, our Mother Earth. This creamy root stew is light and delicate in flavor. Your favorite roots or other vegetables can be substituted for sunroots.*

## For roasted beets

2 medium to large fresh beets, green
    tops reserved (see tip)
1–2 tablespoons oil
1 teaspoon salt
1 teaspoon minced fresh sage + more for serving

## For sunroot stew

3 medium to large sunroots
2 smallish potatoes
green top of 1 leek, remainder reserved
1 tablespoon oil, optional
1 tablespoon salt
2 teaspoons garlic powder
½ teaspoon pepper

## For bison meatballs

1 pound ground bison
½ jalapeño, diced, optional
a few wild leeks, 1 cultivated leek,
    or ½ medium onion, diced
3 portabella or similar wild mushrooms, diced
⅓ cup cooked manoomin
2 tablespoons oil
1½ teaspoons garlic powder
salt and pepper to taste

## For wilted beet greens

green tops of 2 beets, rinsed and
    cut into ½-inch strips
2 cloves garlic, minced
1 tablespoon oil

> TIP: If no beet greens came with your beets, substitute dandelion leaves or other wild edible greens of your choice.

Heat oven to 425 degrees. Remove green tops from beets and set aside (see tip). Scrub beets and cut into quarters, then slice into ⅓-inch-thick pieces. Toss with 1–2 tablespoons oil, 1 teaspoon salt, and 1 teaspoon sage. Place on a small baking sheet and roast for about 20 minutes, then flip beets and continue roasting until tender, about 20 more minutes.

Scrub sunroots and potatoes well, then dice into about 1-inch pieces. Rinse the leek well; cut the green top into large pieces; reserve remainder of leek for meatballs. Place sunroots, potatoes, and leek top in a medium pot with water to cover. Bring to a boil, then reduce heat to medium. Cook for about 20 minutes, stirring occasionally. When sunroots are soft, remove from heat and let cool slightly.

Combine all meatball ingredients (including reserved leek, if using) in a bowl, mixing gently. Shape into 1- to 1½-inch balls and place on a greased baking sheet. Roast at 425 degrees for 5 minutes, flip meatballs, and continue roasting for 5–6 additional minutes.

Remove leek tops from sunroot pot and discard. Drain sunroots and potatoes, reserving liquid. Place sunroots and potatoes in a food processor with 2 cups (or more, for a thinner stew) of the broth. Add 1 tablespoon oil (for smoothness), 1 tablespoon salt, 2 teaspoons garlic powder, and ½ teaspoon pepper. Make sure processor lid is on tight, as contents will be hot. Blend until very smooth. Place back in pot, cover, and keep warm over low heat.

Heat beet greens, garlic, and 1 tablespoon oil in a small pan over medium-high heat for 1–2 minutes, until greens wilt. Remove from heat.

Divide sunroot stew into three bowls, top with meatballs, roasted beets, beet greens, and minced fresh sage. Alternatively, combine everything in the sunroot pot for an evenly colored pink-red stew. Serve hot.

Bison and Sunroot Quick Stew

# American History and the Bison

> "...there's no two ways about it: either the buffalo or the Indian must go. Only when the Indian becomes absolutely dependent on us for his every need, will we be able to handle him. He's too independent with the buffalo. But if we kill the buffalo we conquer the Indian. It seems a more humane thing to kill the buffalo than the Indian, so the buffalo must go."
>
> *The Buffalo Harvest*
> by Frank H. Mayer with Charles B. Roth

I've never been a fan of ground beef. There's something about the gristly texture I've never found agreeable. Ground bison, on the other hand, is much more tender and enjoyable to eat.

I grew up eating hunted, fished, and harvested wild foods. While I loved meat and fish as a youngster, I was also always empathetic toward animals, and at the age of twelve I stopped eating meat altogether until I was twenty-six. As a woman, I quickly noticed the benefits of incorporating wild meats containing iron, like bison and venison, back into my diet; I felt physically stronger within a week, and my hormones and cycle began to even out. The fatty acids in fish are also beneficial during pregnancy, as they help the baby's brain develop.

There are two living species of bison today. The American bison, *Bison bison bison*, and the European wood bison, *Bison bison bonasus*. Both are the largest land mammals of their native land bases. About ninety years ago, *Bison bonasus* were nearly extinct, numbering a mere fifty-four animals total. In 1996 they were classified as an endangered species and are now listed as vulnerable. According to the US Fish and Wildlife Service, there were approximately sixty to seventy million wild bison in North America in the 1500s. By 1884 that number had tragically been reduced to 325, with just twenty-five individuals in Yellowstone National Park.

With efforts to save the bison in the late 1800s, most herds went from being identified with the landscapes they lived upon—north herd, south herd, and so on—to being federal herd, tribal herds, private herds—recognitions indicating ownership and care.

The story of bison involves unexpected twists and turns. Bison were killed by colonizers because bison were and are a source and way of life for Natives. Bison almost went extinct and then were put under conservation laws. Now hunters pay large sums (arguably, sums inaccessible to most Natives) to shoot trophy bison. It is framed that the more hunters who sign up for the lottery to hunt, the better for the conservation efforts because it shows people "value" the bison. This logic has my mind tripping all over itself.

I struggle to understand the values embedded in that worldview—that a person's desire to kill an animal imbues more value than the intrinsic value that animal possesses. Custer State Park in South Dakota has bison trophy hunting. Some people want to hunt bison simply to get a Boone and Crockett record for a big animal they killed. So they can "own" the bison, even in death, apparently. Let me be clear: I am in favor of hunters providing sustenance for their families and communities. It should be noted that only "pure-strain, wild bison" can earn a Boone and Crockett record, because they say killing truly wild things is more of an achievement. I don't have the heart to dive into the whole "Kill the Indian, save the man" government policy parallels here. I'll leave the history of policies to the real history books. (See David Treuer's *The Heartbeat of Wounded Knee*.)

My dad must have been imbued with some strong hunting medicine, because one night he went out to look for moose by himself and came back with one after having stopped his truck along the side of the road and let out a grunt, which brought a moose out of the darkness and right to him. His buddies had refused to go out with him that night, so of course they had to give him a hard time, but they helped clean that moose. He gave away most of the wiiyaas to family, friends, and elders.

# Bison (or Veggie) Crumble Pie

**VEGETARIAN OPTION**      Makes 1 (9-inch) pie or several muffin-sized individual pies

*Serve this savory pie with a side of steamed leafy greens or a favorite garden veggie. You can also adapt this recipe into more of a shepherd's pie, topping it with mashed potatoes in lieu of the crumble before baking. Or try venison, elk, or moose meat instead of bison.*

*The crust is a basic pastry dough with manoomin flour incorporated. The dough will look kind of gray but will start to brown a bit when it's close to done, though not as much as pure wheat pastry dough.*

### For the filling

1 pound ground bison or wiiyaas (meat) of
     choice (or 2 cups diced veggies of choice)
2 cups diced sweet potato
1 cup diced wild leek
2 tablespoons oil
1–2 teaspoons seasoning of choice (I use
     1 teaspoon ground smoked paprika and
     ¼ teaspoon ground chipotle pepper)
1½ teaspoons salt
½ teaspoon maple sugar
water

### For the crust

1½ cups all-purpose flour of choice
½ cup Manoomin Flour (page 35)
½ cup (8 tablespoons) cold butter, diced
1 teaspoon maple sugar
½ teaspoon salt (or more to taste)
6 tablespoons ice water

Cook bison (if using) and veggies in a skillet with oil, seasoning, 1½ teaspoons salt, and ½ teaspoon maple sugar until meat is almost fully cooked and veggies are tender. Add enough water (about 1 cup) to make a gravy, and simmer mixture a few more minutes. The filling should have the consistency of stew or potpie filling. Cover and let cool while you make the crust.

Heat oven to 375 degrees. In a food processor, pulse flours, butter, 1 teaspoon maple sugar, and ½ teaspoon salt until crumbly, then add ice water and pulse several more times until dough forms. Chill dough before pressing into pan—or dive right in if you just can't wait (this is always me!).

Reserve some dough for topping. For a 9-inch pie, press dough into a greased pie pan, fill with filling, and crumble reserved dough on top. For small individual pies, press 1 tablespoon dough into greased muffin pan compartments, add cooled filling to three-quarters full, and sprinkle about 1 tablespoon dough on top, then press down with fingers.

Bake for 30 minutes or until golden brown. If the crumble top is browning quickly or unevenly, reduce heat to 350 degrees for last few minutes.

Serve with your favorite condiments. My husband likes ketchup on his bison crumble pie.

# Sunshine Smoothie

VEGAN, GLUTEN FREE                                                    Serves 2

*A great way to start your morning.*

1 cup carrot juice
1 cup orange juice
a few wild plums, pitted

2 cups Manoomin Milk (page 37),
   frozen in an ice tray
maple syrup to taste

Blend juices, plums, and milk cubes until smooth, adding maple syrup to your preferred sweetness.

*Deanna StandingCloud,*
*Anishinaabe, Red Lake Nation, Community Educator (see bio page 67)*

# Popped Wild Rice Granola Bombs

VEGETARIAN, GLUTEN FREE                                          Makes about 18

*Granola bombs are the perfect nutrient-dense snacks for when a family is on the go. Kids will enjoy making them because everything is mixed in one bowl, the recipe calls for a hands-on approach to shaping them, and the dough is tasty.*

2 cups sunflower butter
1½ cups old fashioned oats
½ cup popped wild rice (page 34)
¼ cup honey

½ cup milk chocolate chips
½ cup chopped pecans
¼ cup chia seeds

Place sunflower butter in a large bowl. Add oats, popped rice, and honey, and stir until batter is firm. Add more oats as needed so that batter comes together. Stir in chocolate chips, pecans, and chia seeds. Using your hands, roll into 1½-inch balls and place on parchment paper. Serve immediately or store in an airtight container in the refrigerator.

# Manoomin Candy

**VEGAN, GLUTEN FREE**                                    Makes 16 (2-inch) squares

*This recipe was inspired by Carl Gawboy, an Anishinaabe painter from Bois Forte, who told me about a kind of candy his mom used to make when he was a boy. I searched through many recipes on the internet and decided to use a nut butter and maple syrup instead of marshmallows to hold the manoomin together. You can make seed or nut butter with whatever seeds or nuts grow in your region. In the Upper Midwest, it might be hazelnut, black walnut, or hickory. Commod peanut butter works too! Add more or less nut butter or maple syrup to suit your preferred gooeyness for these treats. Try adding crushed nuts/seeds, dried fruit bits, or chocolate chips for an even more interesting flavor profile.*

4 cups Popped Manoomin (page 34)
3 tablespoons Puffed
   Amaranth (page 33)
½ cup maple syrup

½ cup peanut butter or other
   seed/nut butter (see note above)
½ teaspoon vanilla or maple extract
dash salt

Grease an 8x8–inch pan or line with parchment paper or silicone mat. Grease a bowl, and pour in popped manoomin and puffed amaranth.

Heat maple syrup and nut butter in a small pot until fragrant and thickening, stirring often. Remove from heat and stir in extract and salt. Drizzle over manoomin and amaranth and stir until well coated. Press mixture into pan. Let cool completely before cutting into squares. Candy will become firmer as it cools; chill in fridge for rapid firming. Store in an airtight container at room temperature.

# Puffed Manoomin Chocolates

VEGETARIAN

*Use as much popped manoomin as you like. For smaller pieces of rice in your candy, use a food processor to crunch up the popped manoomin with a couple of pulses.*

*Get creative with your candy making! Try adding dried flowers, crushed nuts, dried fruit, or candied ginger.*

**Deep-Oil Popped Manoomin (page 34)**
**1 cup chocolate chips or pieces, melted**
**coarse sea salt, optional**

Line a baking sheet with parchment paper or silicone mat. Spread popped manoomin evenly on the baking sheet. Poor melted chocolate evenly over manoomin. Alternatively, mix chocolate and manoomin in a bowl and spread to desired thickness (about ¼ inch) on prepared baking sheet. Sprinkle with coarse sea salt if desired. (Salt causes a dusty whiteness on the top of the chocolate, but I like the flavor.) Let cool on the counter away from the sun (see tip); this could take a few hours. Break into bite-size pieces and store in an airtight container in a cool, dark place.

> **TIP:** If you cool the candy in the fridge, be sure to pull it out as soon as it's set or a white residue may appear on it.

# A Year of Change 2020

I had wanted to learn how to rice in my twenties, but at the time I was occupied with college and working to buy books and such. In 2019 I was able to plan ahead for two weeks off in the summer so I could go out with my dad. As it happened, the manoomin wasn't quite ready until right after that window. It wasn't until the next year that I got a call from my uncle letting me know there was word the manoomin was falling. That year, 2020, was one filled with notable events for me personally and for everyone across the world. I published *Gidjie and the Wolves* in April at the onset of the global pandemic. There was the uprising after the murder of George Floyd. And it was possibly the craziest year for politics. In the fall I went ricing for the first time. I also had my first conversation with binesiwag, the thunderbirds.

My husband and I were staying in Tulsa, Oklahoma, during the winter of 2019–20 when the pandemic started. Our plans to return home that spring were canceled, as travel was not advised. One day early in the pandemic, I lay down after watching the news, which was filled with so much panic and uncertainty. I could hear a very active thunderstorm rolling in, and I had put out my asemaa. As I lay there, I listened to the thunderbeings stop, rumble, and move on from place to place. I listened as they approached our home and stopped right above me. I could see them up there, through the roof, through a hole in the clouds.

Only one talked to me directly. They asked me what my prayer was. I felt around in my heart and soul. I was almost too excited to be having this experience to focus, but I did. I had been writhing in emotional pain before they came. I knew what I wanted to ask for, and I knew it was important that I answer honestly. After I felt all the things I could feel, I asked that the minds, hearts, and spirits of those responsible for making our loved ones disappear would be changed, would be healed so that they wouldn't hurt anyone else, so that our people could heal from their losses and not have to lose any more loved ones.

The thunderbeing who had spoken directly to me told the other thunderbeings what I had said. I could see them too, but they weren't speaking to me. The one then asked me, "Are you sure this is what you want? All of the people around here want this sickness to end." By sickness, I knew they meant COVID-19, and that the people were afraid. I told them I thought the sickness of the minds and spirits of those who were hurting other people was a harder sickness for us to cure ourselves than the ones of the physical body. We have been struggling with this particularly hard-to-cure illness present in our world for so long. I told them, yes, that is my prayer; that is what I am asking for. They accepted my prayer and took it with them, and they moved on, the thunder stopping for a time, then continuing on to another location into the distance.

They visited me once more during the pandemic, while I was in Oklahoma. Not long after their first visit, I wondered if I had asked for the right thing. Had it been selfish to not ask for the whole world to be cured of the COVID-19 virus? Was it selfish to pray so specifically, given such a rare opportunity? I questioned my morals for a time, but I stand by what I asked for that day. Things are moving in a new direction across the world, and I intend to be as intentional as possible with how I interact with creation on all levels. I can only hope to help move things toward a brighter future, in the ways I am able. For those of us who hold no power in the arena of material riches, it's these intimate moments in our interactions with creation that make a difference toward positive change.

# Niibing
## (NEE bihng)

# SUMMER

When you grow up harvesting from lakes and rivers, woodlands and prairies, from the abundance nature provides, you don't particularly characterize these gifts as being "wild." These are simply food. Life.

"We didn't call it foraging," my dad commented during one of our sessions when he was demonstrating how to make ricing push poles.

I, too, didn't know this word *foraging* until I was in college at Bemidji State and heard the term in one of the plant classes I attended. Lifeways for the Anishinaabe that have been fine-tuned over generations are characterized by others as foraging. The word *foraging* for me doesn't carry with it the fine details of how intimate relationships develop between plants and humans. It is nevertheless a word I now use to summarize what I've got going on, when I'd rather not tell someone, "I'm going out to talk to plants today."

Fireworks started going off in my brain as my college professor recited interesting western scientific knowledge about some of the plants. I became acutely aware that a lot of the world doesn't see things the same way the Anishinaabe do. In mainstream botany there are plenty of long names in other languages, old languages. If you ask an Anishinaabe what a plant is called, the answer will probably vary depending on where they live. Not all communities or even individuals within a community know the plants by the same name. The "white flowers of peace" that I knew as such based on a vision and later an actual meeting of these plants is one personal example (see page 8). I knew their name based on how I felt when I met them in all instances. I didn't find out until later that other people knew them as ghost pipe or *Monotropa uniflora* or any other assortment of names. Many plant names are used to convey certain peculiarities that the namer has noticed, based on their personal relationship with the plants or what they personally use them for.

While the translation of the word manoomin (sometimes spelled minoomin) is debatable, I have mostly been told it means "the good berry."

Apart from eating with the seasons, I didn't grow up or live very "traditional." My great-grandmother was the last fluent speaker in our family. She went to a Catholic school and as a result would not speak Anishinaabemowin (Anishinaabe language) in front of us very often, although I'd hear her talking to her mindimooyenyag, old woman friends, on the telephone in the language. I learned some things—how to count, names of animals and such—going to school in Red Lake off and on growing up. I do my best to learn as an adult as I know how much knowledge and worldview is built into the language. And it feels right to learn these things. I am always so thankful for the language teachers in my life who dedicate themselves to helping the rest of us learn.

Like my ancestors, I do, however, pay attention to and honor my dreams. Plants, animals, and other beings have visited me in my dreams to teach me things. My middle-grade book, *Gidjie and the Wolves*, honors these dreams, with the themes and characters of the book, as well as entire written sections, coming from dreams. There's also lots in that book about food and the environment.

The Anishinaabemowin terms used in this book are some that I know and use, and the rest I acquired from the Ojibwe People's Dictionary, available online through the University of Minnesota.

## Watching for the Rice

I love visiting with my friend and Fond du Lac elder and Manoomin Chief Vern Northrup. He loves plants like I do, and I always walk away from our conversations with a little more curiosity and appreciation for the natural world. Because of him, I know that before the snow has all melted, I can watch for the running of maple sap not by tapping the trees myself but by watching the ajida-moog (red squirrels) nibble at the ends of twigs to get a drink. And I never knew that opichiwag (robins) have two broods, one that feeds on worms soon after returning in the spring and another that feeds on juneberries later in the season. These are things you learn when you spend time watching what's going on around you, and I had never seen them myself. It feels like my world expands a little when I hear these details from someone who is patient and observes them firsthand. It is this type of beautiful watching that I admire most in life.

In 2019 Vern and I drove around his rez, and he told me about the history of the dams that still exist there, built on narrow water channels by the local government that wanted to use them to destroy the manoomin in the lakes the people harvest on every year. The local government wanted to destroy the manoomin so that the people would then become farmers. It didn't work. Fond du Lac people to this day are some of the most traditional when it comes to their methods for harvesting manoomin. The people of Fond du Lac now use those same dams once built to destroy their way of life to control the water levels to the benefit of the manoomin and, thus, the people. Manoomin chiefs like Vern watch over the manoomin through the seasons and hold meetings to discuss when it is time to harvest.

Manoomin Chief Vern Northrup shows the dams and waterways of the Fond du Lac reservation.

Dams once built to prevent manoomin harvesting are now used to help maintain best growing conditions for manoomin.

Water flow is monitored on the Fond du Lac reservation.

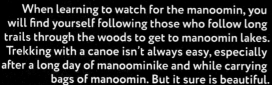
When learning to watch for the manoomin, you will find yourself following those who follow long trails through the woods to get to manoomin lakes. Trekking with a canoe isn't always easy, especially after a long day of manoominike and while carrying bags of manoomin. But it sure is beautiful.

Manoominikaa—much manoomin—is almost ripe at the end of August.

Long, winding dirt roads lead to manoomin. Families check manoomin together.

Watching manoomin at different locations with Kevin Hart Jr., aka Dad

One way to test for ripeness is by bending a few manoomin seeds. If they are milky, they are not ready. This manoomin is still "green."

Dad looks out over a lake full of manoomin. The anticipation is palpable. The harvest is near.

## Tools & Tips for Summer Harvesting

Harvesting wild foods in the summer brings both relief and challenges. Relief in that the harvests can be bountiful, the weather beautiful and inviting. Some of the challenges are fleets of mosquitos, the occasional surprise underground yellow jacket nest, and sun exposure that can sneak up on you and cause dehydration. If you are allergic to bees, go with a friend. Always bring more water than you think you will need. I keep several empty, clean collecting containers in my vehicle and a backpack with essentials like kitchen scissors or shears, a hatchet, a sharp knife, a whistle or bear horn, paper or plastic bags, and, of course, asemaa.

## Common Wild Summer Foods of Minnesota

### Miskominag—Raspberries

Red raspberries are high in antioxidants, fiber, vitamins, and iron, while having low sugar content. Studies show that they have the potential to help lower the risk of diabetes and to lower blood sugar. High in iron, raspberry leaf tea strengthens and tones muscles, eases child labor, increases lactation, and can help reduce cramping during menstruation. The tea stimulates fertility as it balances hormones; it's also good for the skin.

Miskominag can be mistaken for black raspberries that are red when unripe. Unripe black raspberries will not pick easily and will not be tasty. Thimbleberries also resemble red raspberry, but they do not have thorns like raspberry plants do. Thimbleberries have large, maple-like leaves, and go through a beautiful pink stage before they are ripe. Wear a lightweight, long-sleeve shirt when you harvest raspberries to avoid scratches from thorns, and be sure to leave some berries for the makoonsag (bear cubs) and bineshiinyag (birds).

### Miinan—Blueberries

Blueberries are a nutrient-dense food high in antioxidants. Miinan ward off cancer and aging, help improve brain function, and can help protect you from bacterial infection. They grow on shrubs and turn from a pale green to a beautiful fuchsia and finally to blue when ripe. Bushes can have berries of all hues at the same time. If they are tiny and blue and you have to tug at them, wait a couple of days and check them again. The berries will swell in size and come off the stem easily when they are ready to eat. They are similar to huckleberries, but blueberries have a powdery appearance whereas huckleberries do not. Miinan ripen before chokecherries.

### Ozigwaakominag—Juneberries

In mid-July the juneberry harvest is in full swing across the Midwest. In some places, like Minneapolis and central Wisconsin, the harvest might have been waning for weeks, while in slightly more northern latitudes, like Bemidji, folks might be bush-side, buckets in hand, still eagerly awaiting peak plumpness.

The unassuming and often overlooked juneberry is known fondly by many names: serviceberry, sarviceberry, shadbush, saskatoon—the list goes on. Ozigwaakominag is how people I know refer to these sweet, almost "meaty" fruits.

Juneberries are a good source of iron, full of anthocyanins, and versatile when it comes to culinary adventure. They make wonderful jams, jellies, pies, and syrup, and they are a great counterpoint when combined with savory elements.

### Asasaweminan—Chokecherries

The dark color of a chokecherry is attributed to antioxidants, which help reduce excess inflammation and lower the risk of cancer. They also protect your heart and

Be prepared: keep a backpack with containers in it with you at all times during berry season.

Jelly jars are good for a berry harvest on the go.

Young raspberry plants grow amidst prior years' brambles.

Ripe red raspberries

Unripe black raspberry resembles red raspberry.

liver. Asasaweminan have fiber, vitamins C and K, and manganese, and the inner bark of the chokecherry tree is used for the relief of menstrual cramps. They are known as "drupe fruits," which have a stone pit that carries the seed. They are harvested in mid- to late summer, after most of the other fruits. When ripe they are dark purple or nearly black. They are tart and mildly sweet; eaten raw, they make your mouth pucker. Because of this tartness, chokecherries make excellent syrup and jam.

### Odatagaagominag—Blackberries

I am always fascinated by the strong visual presence of blackberry brambles. With their sturdy, vinelike stems and thick thorns, they are not in the least bit shy about claiming space. I find this way of presenting themselves admirable. Unripe blackberries, red in color, are distinguishable from red raspberries in that raspberries are shaped like a cup while blackberries are solid throughout.

Ripening blueberries

The beautiful shades blueberries go through on their way to ripeness

Juneberries start to form just after the flowers have fallen.

Juneberries

Near-ripe chokecherries. *Photo by Ivy Vainio*

Chokecherry flowers, and thus the fruits, form in arrangements called *racemes*.

Unripe blackberries. Brambles are thick and have thorns.

Ripening thimbleberries

## Thimbleberries
This plant called to me by the rivers in the Duluth area, and I have since learned about thimbleberries over the course of a few years. This is one of the plants that has connected me to other people through dreams. It never fails to amaze me how plants reach out to us, to have relationships with us and even bring us together.

## Blue Jays, Moose, and Reaching for Healing

**DIARY, JULY 10, 2019**

The blue jays called from the cedar tree. I looked out the half-opened window to see two parents and a young one hopping around. The young one and I shared views of each other. I made my sound and offered connective ways. I went outside and made my sound for a minute or so. I felt they had come to visit. I returned inside and the sun came out. Jewels of sunlit drizzle made their way to the earth. Within minutes the sky was blue once again; white, fluffy clouds moving through, the birds singing in the distance. The family of blue jays moved on through the day, eager and proud to show the world to and share connections with their youngster.

I sit on the couch thinking about healing. The blue jays' visit brought some moments of healing from the loss of my pregnancy. I think about a friend who is still unconscious a few days after having brain surgery to repair an aneurism. I wonder how I might offer service and help bring healing through this world. As I sit in my house in the middle of Lakeside, Duluth, I begin to hear the calling of not one but multiple moose to the south, where I know there are more neighborhoods the same as here, more houses with mowed lawns. But looking inside, I see moose wading in swamp and marsh water, those plants and that environment, and they are calling out. I feel the moose are great healers. And their calls do bring in a song of healing. As with any intimate visit from plant or animal beings, I feel humbled to have moose visit me on occasion. In one dream I saw a female moose swimming between floating plants in a boggy area. She was eating plants in the water and had plant medicine in her mouth. And she was following a canoe with people in it.

Photo by Aaron Doucett, unsplash.com

**PLANT DIARY, AUGUST 28, 2019**

I was foraging out in the woods today off an old dirt road that has thick swatches of hazelnut bushes right up to the edges of each side of the road, which is just wide enough for two cars to edge past each other if they're careful. It's a community of hazelnut shrubs I've happily visited before. It's always so peaceful out there.

I had been harvesting for maybe an hour when I was distinctly told by the hazelnut bushes themselves that I should get in my car because there was going to be another car coming. Right after I got into my car, I looked in my rearview mirror and could see a vehicle come into view down the road, which went straight back for a ways. The hazelnuts let me know someone was coming because they know I don't like harvesting when other people are around. I like to have quietness to connect with the plants I am harvesting, and the energy of other people is usually too chaotic for me to fully immerse myself in what I'm doing.

It was really windy out there, and I couldn't hear the sound of the car engine until it got really close to me. When the hazelnuts spoke to me, it wasn't exactly words, but more like they were sending the feeling of what it's like for that car to come down that road at that time. I understood at once and made my way out of the bush and back to the road. As a woman alone out in the woods, I don't like to feel like I can't see when people are approaching me. And the hazelnut bushes understood this and communicated with me based on my needs, shared in my thoughts, intentions, prayers, and direct conversations with them.

Hazelnuts growing with blackberries

## Learning to Pole
**AUGUST 2020**

"Canoes are like the Ojibwe bicycle; once you learn how to ride one, you'll never forget," Niiyawen'enh and uncle tells me during his demo for me, my husband, and a few other people on how to pole in a canoe for the first time on the Mississippi River on one fine, sunny August day in 2020.

He pushes off from shore and quickly makes his way in circles and up and down the river in front of us, crossing multiple times through the fast-moving current in the middle. He comes back to the shore with a big smile on his face and then sets us loose in pairs. "Don't fall in!" he tells us, chuckling.

Now, I'd been in a canoe many times, but I had always used paddles, never a ricing push pole. The thing about pushing a canoe with one of these poles is you have to be standing up. And while standing, you have to be able to maneuver the pole around your back. You also must perform all sorts of tricky moves to leverage your weight and keep the canoe on track and in rhythm with your knocker, the person sitting down knocking the manoomin into the canoe, while also not tipping the canoe over. This requires firmly planted feet, strong legs and arms, and an abdomen of steel.

River poling isn't easy, especially on the Mississippi, where the current can move fast and powerfully. Such was the case on that day. As I wove and spun through the water, my heart pounded and my hands gripped that pole tightly, tighter than they'd ever gripped anything before. I was afraid to let go for one second. It was in those moments of adrenaline and determination, with the sunlight shining down on me, that I felt my ancestors singing their own experiences of thrill-filled joy, making all the cells in my body buzz and vibrate with pure happiness, causing me to feel like I had been born to pole in a canoe.

> "There's a lot to developing your canoe legs. They always told me not to look at the sky while I'm poling, because you get disoriented and flip the canoe over."
>
> —Kevin Hart Jr.

Knockers are lightweight so they don't bust up the manoomin.

# Blueberry Manoomin Milk

VEGAN, GLUTEN FREE                                                    Serves 2

½ cup blueberries
½ cup water
1½ cups Manoomin Milk (page 37)

1–2 tablespoons blueberry syrup
pinch salt

Place blueberries and water in a small saucepan and bring to a boil. Reduce heat to low; cover and let simmer 5 minutes. Stir in milk, blueberry syrup, and salt and heat just until hot, stirring often. Blend in a food processor until smooth. Add extra milk or water to reach preferred consistency. Strain if desired. Serve over ice.

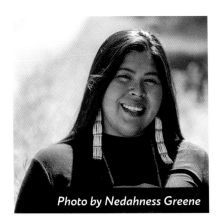

*Photo by Nedahness Greene*

*Awanook Veronica Kingbird-Bratvold,*
*Anishinaabekwe, Red Lake Nation Ojibwe*

**MEd,** *University of Minnesota Duluth; Cultural*
*Coordinator, Ombimindwaa Gidinawemaaganinaadog*

# Wiishkobi-Manoomin (Sweet Wild Rice)

VEGAN, GLUTEN FREE                    Serves 3–5

*Awanook Veronica Kingbird-Bratvold is a band member of the Red Lake Nation who lives and works in the Red Lake School District. Veronica grew up learning about medicines and ceremonial practices in her household. She has continued learning from the community as an adult and has a passion for sharing cultural knowledge with others in order to conserve Anishinaabeg lifeways and maintain identities and connectedness. She enjoys harvesting wild foods, helping people with pets, rescuing rez dogs, four wheeling, cooking, and spending time with her family and pets.*

*I admire Veronica's hard work toward making our nation a happy and healthy place for all to live. She volunteers her time, energy, and resources for the causes she believes in and inspires others to follow. And to top it off, she is one of the friendliest people I know. I am so happy to be able to share her recipe for Wiishkobi-Manoomin (Sweet Wild Rice) with you noongom (today).*

1 cup miinan (blueberries)
½ cup miskomiinan
    (raspberries)
2 cups ode'iminan
    (strawberries),
    hulled and sliced
½ cup odatagaagominag
    (blackberries)

2 cups cooked and cooled
    manoomin (wild rice)
seeds from
    1 pomegranate (see tip)
¼ cup zhiiwaagamizigan
    (maple syrup)
2 tablespoons chopped mint
zenziibaakwad (maple sugar)

Rinse and pat dry all berries. Place manoomin in a serving dish or bowl and add all fruit. Gradually drizzle and fold zhiiwaagamizigan into the manoomin-berry mixture. Garnish with mint and zenziibaakwad.

**TIP:** To seed a pomegranate, cut off the top part, then slice into quarters. Set fruit into a dish of cool water and pry out the seeds. The pulp will float: skim and discard.

# Manoomin Parfait to Go

*This recipe makes for a healthy, delicious lunch or snack on the go.*

mason jar or other container with a lid
Manoomin Pie Crust mixture
   (page 40) made without water

yogurt or pudding of choice
Wiishkobi-Manoomin (page 95)
fresh fruit

Put about 1–2 tablespoons of the crumbly pie crust mixture in the bottom of the jar. Layer in some yogurt, Wiishkobi-Manoomin, more yogurt, fruit, and more seed mixture. Create as many layers as you like for a jar of delicious, nutritious adventure fuel!

Wiishkobi-Manoomin (page 95). *Image courtesy Veronica Bratvold*

# Chagaccino with Currant, Raspberry, Maple, and Manoomin Milk

VEGAN, GLUTEN FREE                                    Serves 2–4

*Summer raspberries are found in abundance in the Midwest. This drink is great to sip on cool evenings while you study the Manidoo Miikana (River of Souls, Milky Way galaxy).*

2 cups Manoomin Milk (page 37)
   or milk of choice
¼ cup dried currants

½ cup fresh red raspberries (see tip)
2 cups strong hot chaga tea
¼ cup maple syrup

In a medium saucepan heat milk, currants, and raspberries over medium-low heat until fruit softens. Stir in tea and maple syrup, then blend with an immersion blender until smooth and frothy. Add more maple syrup if desired. Serve hot.

> **TIP:** If you don't like raspberry seeds, choose a different fruit. The immersion blender will bust down some of the seeds, but there will still be some pieces that settle to the bottom of your chagaccino.

Chaga grows on paper birch trees and has long been utilized medicinally across the globe. I tend to harvest more often during seasons when there are fewer leaves, which makes chaga easier to spot. The flavor of chaga is difficult to describe; when it is simmered for a few hours to allow the flavor to develop, to me it is reminiscent of chocolate mixed with molasses and a hint of woody earthiness. You can also find chaga in many health food stores. Don't overindulge, but do enjoy responsibly.

Cow parsnip flowers emerging

Young cow parsnip. I like to harvest the leaves when they're a little smaller than this, about six inches long. The plants pictured are about a foot tall. I love the flavor of the leaves. Some people might not find it agreeable; as with any good seasoning herb it has a distinct flavor, and you'll probably either love it or hate it.

End-of-season cow parsnip

# Cow Parsnip
This is a plant you absolutely must learn to identify with a guide in person to understand the potential hazards that come with harvest protocols. There are also some look-alikes that you don't want to mistake for cow parsnip, like water hemlock. Take precautions when harvesting young leaves and stalks, as some people have negative reactions after getting the juice on their skin and then being exposed to sunlight. I have never had any problems with this plant myself in that regard, but I do take care to not get the juice on me as I harvest, and I don't eat any part of it until I'm indoors. I know people who eat the roots too, but I have no experience with that.

# Creamy Coconut Garden Veggies and Bison over Manoomin

**GLUTEN FREE**                                                              Serves 4

2 tablespoons oil
1 pound ground bison or
    2 cups diced veggies
2 small summer squash, chopped
    into ⅓-inch cubes
½ cup chopped broccoli
½ cup + 3 tablespoons coconut milk
1 tablespoon sea salt

1 teaspoon ground turmeric
1 teaspoon herb blend (for example,
    parsley, wild bergamot, rosemary,
    garden sage, or cow parsnip)
pinch sugar
4 cups hot cooked manoomin
3 tablespoons shredded Romano cheese

Heat oil in large skillet over medium heat. Add bison (or diced veggies) and cook, covered, for 5 minutes, occasionally breaking up ground bison with spatula and allowing condensation from the lid to drip back down into the pan as you work.

Add squash, broccoli, ½ cup coconut milk, salt, turmeric, herb blend, and sugar to the bison. Cook for 3 minutes at a medium to medium-low simmer. Don't let mixture boil or the coconut milk will lose some of its flavor.

Stir in manoomin and increase heat to medium-high. Cook for 3 minutes. Reduce heat to medium for another minute, sprinkle cheese on top, cover, and remove from heat. After a few minutes, stir in remaining 3 tablespoons coconut milk and mix well with the cheese. Serve hot.

# Milkweed Stir-Fry

VEGETARIAN, GLUTEN FREE                                                    Serves 4

⅓ cup sliced almonds
2 tablespoons butter
1 cup milkweed pods (2 inches in
    length or smaller), parboiled,
    then halved lengthwise

1 cup chopped wild edible mushroom
    (cultivated is great too)
3 cloves garlic, minced
1–2 tablespoons low-sodium
    soy sauce, to taste
2 cups cooked manoomin

In a dry skillet over medium heat, lightly toast almonds just until they begin to smell fragrant, stirring to avoid burning. Increase heat to medium-high and add butter, parboiled milkweed pods, mushrooms, garlic, and soy sauce. Cook for 3–5 minutes, until mushrooms wilt and brown, then stir in manoomin. Cook until hot; serve immediately.

Edible common milkweed fruit pods at just the right size for harvesting

Make sure your pods are completely white on the inside, with no black specks. Be sure to leave plenty of milkweed pods on the plants so seeds can mature for next year.

Manoomin à la "Something Else"

# Manoomin à la "Something Else"

VEGAN, GLUTEN FREE                                                    Serves 3–6

*This dish is bursting with a diversity of flavor, color, and texture—just like Indigenous people. Feel free to substitute your favorite veggies or stir in some meat as you see fit.*

3 tablespoons oil
1½ cups halved baby potatoes, skins on
1½ cups halved brussels sprouts
1½ cups thick-shredded purple cabbage
1 small onion, diced
½ tablespoon red pepper flakes, optional

1 cup shredded carrot
1 cup cooked hominy
1–2 tablespoons water
salt to taste
1 cup cooked manoomin
1 tablespoon chokecherry syrup

Heat oil in a large skillet on medium heat and add potatoes. Cook, covered, for 4 minutes, then stir in brussels sprouts, cabbage, onion, and red pepper flakes (if using). Cook another 2 minutes, then add the carrot and hominy. Cook a minute or two, until the hominy is hot, and then add in water and salt. Cook, covered, until the potatoes are softened but not mushy and brussels sprouts are nicely browned. Stir in the manoomin and chokecherry syrup and heat, uncovered, for 1 minute. Serve hot.

# Avocado Salad

VEGAN, GLUTEN FREE Serves 2–3

*Chilled cooked rice will give your salad more texture. For a softer texture, either use fresh cooked and cooled rice or bring refrigerated rice to room temperature before mixing. Pair this salad with savory Manoomin Breakfast Pies (page 66) for a tasty brunch combo.*

2 cups cooked manoomin (chilled or at room temperature)
⅓ cup diced tomato
2 tablespoons diced wild or cultivated onion
1 tablespoon chopped cilantro

1 teaspoon minced jalapeño
1 teaspoon minced garlic, optional
squeeze lime
salt to taste
1 avocado, diced

Stir together all ingredients, adding avocado last. Serve cool, warm, or at room temperature.

Avocado Salad

# Nutty Manoomin Patties with Ogaa (Walleye) Cheeks and Fiddlehead-Nettle Puree

GLUTEN FREE                                                                 Serves 2–4

*The puree in this recipe is similar to a kale pesto my friend and colleague Vern DeFoe developed for the Tatanka Truck menu. I adapted his recipe to incorporate wild greens. When making the puree, feel free to throw in roasted garlic or leeks—whatever you want to add flavor. There's a lot of oil in this puree, so think of it as a condiment, not a vegetable side dish. This recipe makes a fairly good-sized batch—and once you have it, you might find yourself putting it on just about anything. Think breakfast burritos, salads, sandwiches, etc. Store any leftover puree in the fridge.*

1 cup shelled pumpkin seeds
   or other seeds or nuts
1 tablespoon powdered sumac, or
   substitute a squeeze of lemon
2 cups blanched fiddlehead ostrich
   ferns, or whatever is local to you

2 cups blanched stinging nettles
   or other wild green(s)
1 cup + 1–2 tablespoons neutral oil
salt
1 pound walleye cheeks
Nutty Manoomin Patties (page 62)

In a food processor, blend pumpkin seeds, sumac, fiddleheads, nettles, and about 1 cup oil until smooth, seasoning with salt to taste. You should be able to squeeze puree out of a squeeze bottle or drip it from a spoon, but make sure it's not too runny. Set aside.

Rinse walleye cheeks in cold water, checking for and removing any hard pieces that might be stuck to them. Put 1–2 tablespoons oil (or butter) in a skillet over medium heat (see tip) and add cheeks. Cook, covered, until cheeks are soft, stirring occasionally. Season with salt to taste.

Top manoomin patties with fiddlehead-nettle puree, ogaa cheeks, and any favorite wild garnishes.

> **TIP:** If you don't want to use butter or oil to cook the walleye cheeks, steam them instead. Pour enough water into the pan so they don't stick, but not so much as to make it runny like soup.

Harvesting young nettles

## Stinging Nettles
Stinging nettles are delicious when steamed, make a nutritious tea, and also dehydrate well. Young leaves in spring are best for harvesting. Do not attempt to eat stinging nettle raw.

Bison and Wild Rice–Stuffed Grape Leaves. *Image courtesy Marisa Lee*

Wild grapes have simple, palmate-shaped leaves.

Virginia creeper

Wild grapes

## Virginia Creeper

Virginia creeper, shown here, is often mistaken for wild grape because they are both crawling vines that have dark, round fruit. Notice how the leaves of Virginia creeper are compound with five leaflets per leaf, whereas the leaves of wild grape are simple and resemble maple leaves.

**Image courtesy Marisa Lee**

*Marisa Lee is a recent law school graduate and self-described plant nerd. A descendant of Red Lake Nation and Oneida Nation of Wisconsin, she's particularly interested in learning how people and plants take care of each other. I enjoy talking with Marisa about plants and feel a special bond with her as we are both Red Lakers. I was happy to see her recipe involving grape leaves, as I've been wanting to wrap up all manner of things in them for years. Here in the Upper Midwest we are blessed with lots of wild grapes.*

**TIP:** A good how-to video, "How to Make Dolmas," can be found here: https://youtu.be/bq5lwrZkEjk. Marisa says, "I used this technique to learn how to roll and cook these, and it didn't let me down."

*Marisa Lee*

# Bison and Wild Rice–Stuffed Grape Leaves

GLUTEN FREE                                        Makes about 50

*This recipe is an Indigenous take on traditional dolmades. As written, all ingredients are indigenous to the Americas, but it's a very adaptable recipe. Feel free to substitute. Use the oil and seasonings you have on hand, and consider replacing the raisins with dried currants, dried blueberries, sunflower seeds, or pumpkin seeds. Have fun with it.*

1 pound ground bison
1 cup wild rice
¼ cup grapeseed oil + more to drizzle into pan
¼ cup golden raisins

2 teaspoons salt
1 teaspoon allspice
2 sprigs fresh tarragon, chopped
2 (16-ounce) jars grape leaves
8 cups broth

In a medium bowl combine meat, wild rice, oil, raisins, salt, allspice, and tarragon, mixing gently. Cover and set aside.

Drain grape leaves and ease leaf bundle out of each jar. Submerge in a bowl of water to gently separate the leaves. Make a stack of whole leaves and another stack of badly ripped or partial leaves; do not discard damaged leaves.

On a large work surface, lay out as many leaves as will fit without overlapping, smooth side down. Scoop a rounded tablespoon of filling into the center of each leaf. Fold bottom of leaf over filling, fold in sides, then roll toward tip of leaf. Do not overfill or roll tightly; filling will expand with cooking. Continue until all are filled and rolled.

Prepare a large pot by oiling the bottom and lining with damaged leaves. Place stuffed grape leaves in a layer, close together but not packed tightly. Use additional damaged leaves to create a barrier before placing a second layer of stuffed grape leaves.

Cover with broth, just to the top of the grape leaves and not higher. If the broth does not quite cover, add water. Weigh down the grape leaves to hold them in place, for instance with an inverted saucer under an inverted plate.

Cover and simmer about 1 hour. Do not boil. Remove plates carefully with tongs and use a fork to test for doneness. If needed, continue to simmer but do not replace the plates.

Remove cooked grape leaves from hot broth using tongs. Serve hot, at room temperature, or cold. Chill and slice in half with a sharp knife for truly bite-size finger food.

# Cauliflower Manoomin Breakfast Muffins

VEGETARIAN, GLUTEN FREE                                            Makes 12 muffins

*These muffins are packed with good energy to start your day off right. Kids and picky spouses won't even know there is cauliflower in them. Shh…*

1 cup fresh cauliflower chunks
1 cup cooked, cooled manoomin
2 tablespoons diced wild leeks or onion

¼ cup chopped wild or farmed spinach
½ teaspoon salt
6 eggs, beaten

Heat oven to 350 degrees. Grease a muffin pan (or leave ungreased if silicone; see tip).

Pulse cauliflower in a food processor until it looks similar to powdered Parmesan cheese; you should have about 1 loose cup of cauliflower bits. Place cauliflower in a bowl and stir in manoomin, leeks/onion, spinach, and salt. Spoon a heaping tablespoon of the mixture into each muffin compartment. Beat eggs in a liquid measuring cup and pour over the muffin mixture. Bake for 20 minutes or until the tops are firm and the sides start to pull away from the pan. Cool slightly and enjoy.

**TIP:** If you're using a silicone pan, put it on a metal baking sheet before popping in the oven.

Cauliflower Manoomin Breakfast Muffins

Cauliflower pieces should be tiny.

# Easy Manoomin and Bison Stir-Fry

Serves 3–4

*This straightforward, delicious, and nutritious meal is quick and easy to make and sure to satisfy. I suggest you put on a bib and chow down on the couch so you can fall asleep full and happy afterward. We sure did!*

1 pound ground bison
½ small onion, diced
1 red bell pepper, diced
½ head broccoli, diced

1 cup sliced mushrooms
4 eggs, optional
seasonings to taste
2 cups cooked manoomin

In a large skillet, cook bison and onion with a little oil until bison is starting to brown. Add bell pepper, broccoli, and mushrooms; cover pan and let cook 4–5 minutes, stirring every couple minutes. Stir in eggs (if using) and seasonings of choice. When veggies start to soften and bison is cooked through, stir in manoomin, reduce heat, and cook, covered, for 2 minutes.

Easy Manoomin and Bison Stir-Fry

*Image courtesy Sean Sherman*

*Sean Sherman, Oglala Lakota, is dedicated to raising awareness and understanding around Indigenous foodways. In 2014 he opened the Sioux Chef as a catering and food education initiative in the Minneapolis–St. Paul area with menus featuring regional Indigenous foods. In 2018 his book, The Sioux Chef's Indigenous Kitchen, won the James Beard Award for Best American Cookbook. That same year, Sean cofounded North American Traditional Indigenous Food Systems (NāTIFS), a nonprofit dedicated to addressing some of the health and economic suffering in Native communities. In 2020 NāTIFS opened the Indigenous Food Lab in Minneapolis as an education and research hub that will help cultivate a new generation of Indigenous food leaders while working to steward Indigenous food knowledge for generations to come.*

*Sean created this recipe during a live demo at the Minnesota State Fair. It is similar to the manoomin bowls our Tatanka Truck crew was slinging to hungry downtowners in Minneapolis back in 2016 before the big bison retired. I love that this dish tastes like a celebration of different seasons.*

*Sean Sherman, founder/CEO, the Sioux Chef / NāTIFS; Indigenous culinary director, Indigenous Food Lab; board member, Dream of Wild Health / Seed Savers Exchange*

# Minnesota Wild Rice and Veggie Bowl

VEGAN, GLUTEN FREE                                    Serves 2–3

*Feel free to substitute any ingredient or add protein of choice.*

2 tablespoons sunflower oil
¼ cup minced leek
¼ cup minced turnip
¼ cup minced squash
2 cups cooked wild rice

¼ cup maple syrup
½ cup water
1 tablespoon smoked salt
¼ cup sunflower seeds

## Toppings

1 squash blossom, halved lengthwise
2 medium crab apples, cored, seeded, and cut into bite-size pieces
¼ cup snap peas
2 summer squash (patty pan), diced

3 tablespoons Popped Amaranth (page 33)
½ cup sliced wild greens (dandelion, purslane, plantain, etc.)
½ cup blackberries smashed with a fork

Heat oil in a skillet, then add leek, turnip, and squash and cook, stirring. Stir in wild rice and add maple syrup, water, and salt. Simmer until liquid is reduced, then stir in sunflower seeds and remove from heat.

Heat a cast iron skillet, then add squash blossoms, crab apples, snap peas, and summer squash to caramelize.

Place wild rice mix in bottom of serving bowl, and artfully arrange other ingredients on top of rice. Serve hot and enjoy while contemplating the history of the land you currently reside on.

**Image courtesy Awanigiizik Bruce**

Awanigiizhik Bruce is a citizen of the Turtle Mountain Pembina Chippewa Nation. They are a diverse media artist, tribal community leader, strategic planner, networker, tour guide, and volunteer and also a senior in the bachelor's program of Ojibwe Language, Culture, and History at Turtle Mountain Community College. One of the prominent art forms Awanigiizhik uses—out of around thirty different ones—is the art and science (chemistry) of cooking. They have been cooking for their family since the age of five.

I met Awanigiizhik at an art and craft fair in Red Lake and have been a fan ever since. One of the most creative and generously knowledgeable people I know, Awanigiizhik has put that creativity to work crafting some tasty recipes to share with us.

*Awanigiizhik Bruce, Turtle Mountain Band of Chippewa Indians of North Dakota*

# Wild Rice and Blueberry Waffles

Serves 4

*Boozhoo gakina awiya! Welcome everyone! This recipe is one of my favorites to make for family and friends for breakfast. Wild rice waffles are versatile, tasty, and healthy. You can add different ingredients to customize this recipe. The flavor profile can be savory, sweet, salty, etc. Please enjoy and make this recipe a family favorite from mine to yours.*

2 cups all-purpose flour
2 teaspoons baking powder
½ teaspoon salt
4 eggs, separated
2 tablespoons sugar
½ teaspoon vanilla extract
4 tablespoons unsalted butter, melted

2 cups milk
1½ cups cooked wild rice
1 cup wild blueberries +
    more for serving
½ cup chopped pecans
maple syrup for serving
mint leaves for garnish, optional

Preheat waffle iron. In a bowl sift together flour, baking powder, and salt; set aside.

In a large bowl, beat egg yolks and sugar until sugar is completely dissolved and eggs are pale yellow. Whisk in vanilla, melted butter, and milk. Add flour mixture and whisk until just blended. Do not overmix.

In another bowl, beat egg whites with an electric mixer until soft peaks form, about 1 minute. Use a rubber spatula to gently fold egg whites into the waffle batter. Do not overmix. Gently fold in wild rice, blueberries, and pecans.

Coat the waffle iron with nonstick cooking spray and pour in enough batter to just cover waffle grid. Close the waffle iron and cook until waffles are golden brown, about 2–3 minutes. Serve immediately, topped with your favorite flavor: maple syrup, fresh blueberries, and maybe some mint leaves. Enjoy!

Miigwech sa dago mii'iw! Thank you and that's all!

Blueberry Blue Corn Pancakes

# Blueberry Blue Corn Pancakes

*I enjoy the flavor and texture of these pancakes all by themselves and like to snack on them once they're cooled. I used the recipe for waffles on the back of the Bow & Arrow blue cornmeal package as a leaping-off point for this recipe. Serve with your favorite syrup or top with an over-medium egg. Heck: why not do both?*

3 eggs
1⅓ cups milk (almond or other)
1 cup all-purpose flour
½ cup Manoomin Flour (page 35)
½ cup blue cornmeal
2 tablespoons maple sugar

¼ teaspoon baking powder
¼ teaspoon salt
⅓ cup cooked, cooled manoomin
⅓ cup + 1 tablespoon frozen
   wild blueberries

Beat eggs with milk and set aside. Whisk together flours, cornmeal, maple sugar, baking powder, and salt in a large bowl, then stir in the eggs and milk just until smooth. Stir in manoomin and blueberries. Portion cakes to cook in a lightly oiled pan over medium heat until the bubbles in the middle are popped and the edges are dry (about 3 minutes). Flip and cook another 2–3 minutes. Store leftovers in the refrigerator for a few days in an airtight container.

# Wild Blueberry Pan Breads

Serves 2

*These pan breads are a wheat-free, delicious alternative to biscuits. Serve with jam.*
*To enjoy for breakfast, make the dough the night before.*

⅓ cup manoomin
⅓ cup frozen wild blueberries
   (or other fruit, diced)
1½ cups water + more as needed
1½ tablespoons maple sugar

1 tablespoon oil
pinch salt
4–5 tablespoons Manoomin
   Flour (page 35)

In a small pot, stir together manoomin, blueberries, and water. Cook, loosely covered, over medium heat until rice is soft, about 30 minutes, adding more water as needed. Let cool until safe to handle.

In a food processor or blender, combine rice and berry blend, maple sugar, oil, and salt. Blend until smooth. Pour mixture in bowl and stir in just enough flour to make a sticky dough the consistency of thick oatmeal. Allow dough to cool, then put in a sealed container and refrigerate until morning (or at least a couple of hours).

Lightly grease a skillet and set over medium heat. Using about 1 tablespoon of dough, make small patties, 1½ inch wide by about ½ inch thick. Cook about 3 minutes on each side, until breads are nicely browned. Serve warm.

Wild Blueberry Pan Breads

Maple Cauliflower Pie

# Maple Cauliflower Pie

VEGETARIAN, GLUTEN FREE                                          Makes 1 (9-inch) pie

*This pie is reminiscent of the eggy bread pudding my mom would make us as kids. If you like eggy custard, you just might love this pie! The cauliflower taste is subtle and complementary yet intriguing: people will ask what the secret ingredient is. If you want to get adventurous, try swapping out the cauliflower with zucchini, summer squash, or a combination of the three. For an even more interesting burst of flavor, try drizzling this pie with Rose Sauce (page 153) or caramel (page 201).*

1½ cups sweet potato puree (see below)
1 cup cauliflower puree (see below)
¾ cup + 3–4 tablespoons maple sugar
1 teaspoon vanilla extract
1 teaspoon salt

½ cup coconut milk or Manoomin
    Milk (page 37)
3 tablespoons Manoomin
    Flour (page 35)
3 eggs

Heat oven to 350 degrees and lightly grease the bottom and sides of a 9x2¾-inch springform pan.

In a medium bowl, mix sweet potato puree, cauliflower puree, ¾ cup maple sugar, vanilla, salt, milk, and flour. Beat eggs in a separate bowl and then stir into the mixture until just blended. Pour batter into prepared pan and sprinkle 3–4 tablespoons maple sugar on top. Bake 45 minutes or until tester comes out clean and the edges have pulled away from the pan. Cool before serving.

## Sweet Potato Puree

Heat oven to 350 degrees. Peel and dice 2 large sweet potatoes. Toss with a drizzle of oil and pinch of salt. Roast on a baking sheet 25 minutes or until soft. Let cool, then blend in a food processor until smooth.

## Cauliflower Puree

Chop enough cauliflower in grape-size pieces to fill 2 cups. Place in a small pot with a little water and steam until soft but still with texture, about 5 minutes. Drain and blend in a food processor until smooth.

# Ginger Maple Sugar Manoomin Dust

VEGAN, GLUTEN FREE

*A flavorful sprinkle for your favorite homemade coffee drinks, ice cream, oatmeal, roasted squash, and fresh-cut fruit. Change the ratio to suit your taste; add salt and other powdered spices as you like. Or get fancy and add crushed dried flowers.*

2 tablespoons + 2 teaspoons maple sugar
2 teaspoons toasted Manoomin Flour (page 35)
1 teaspoon ground ginger

Measure into a lidded jar and shake to combine.

Juneberries

# Spiced Juneberry Muffins

VEGETARIAN                                                    Makes 6 muffins

*One day, at the tail end of winter, I had been daydreaming about making juneberry muffins and out of nowhere I got a text from Heid E. Erdrich detailing how she had some frozen juneberries she'd wanted to give me. This recipe was developed thanks to those two friends—Heid and the juneberry. For extra texture and flavor, add 3 tablespoons Puffed Amaranth (page 33). Delicious served warm with a dab of butter. For a special treat, pair with Baby Yoda's Favorite Hot Choccy (page 187).*

1½ cups all-purpose flour
½ cup Manoomin Flour (page 35)
½ cup maple sugar
½ cup granulated sugar
1 teaspoon ground cinnamon
1 teaspoon ground ginger
1 teaspoon ground nutmeg
pinch salt

1 cup milk of choice
⅓ cup oil
2 eggs
½ cup (8 tablespoons) butter, melted
½ cup juneberries (frozen or fresh)
Ginger Maple Sugar Manoomin
     Dust (page 122)

Heat oven to 350 degrees. Grease muffin pan (or leave ungreased if using a silicone pan; see tip page 110).

In a bowl, stir together flours, sugars, spices, and salt. In a large fluid measuring cup, measure milk and oil, and then lightly beat in eggs. Stir milk mixture and butter into dry ingredients until just mixed. Fold in juneberries.

Fill muffin compartments to about ½ inch from top of pan and sprinkle tops with Ginger Maple Sugar Manoomin Dust. Bake until a tester comes out clean, about 15–17 minutes. Let cool a bit before serving.

# Dagwaaging
(dug WAH gihng)

# FALL

In the past, dagwaaging was for me largely characterized by the harvest of bagaanag, hazelnuts, as they tend to grow in large patches and make for a substantial harvest. Thanks to the help of family and friends, I now have another bountiful harvest to look forward to: manoomin.

## Ricing Medicine in a Pandemic

It was in the middle of the coronavirus pandemic when I met up with my relatives to go harvest rice for the first time. I thought about whether it was a good idea for me to be around other people. Was it selfish to try to learn at that time? In a canoe you are outside and at least six feet apart. I reasoned that it was safe enough, and so I went.

It was good medicine for me, learning how to rice during a pandemic. At a time when the world seemed to be on fire, I found peace and strength out on that water. Intentions have been formed and, much like a poler pulls and pushes the canoe along on the water, I can feel my intentions pulling and pushing me into the future, strengthening my hope for our collective healing. That's what it feels like out there: joy, hope, strength, connection, and healing.

## Tools & Tips for Fall Harvesting

As the abundance of wild summer foods comes to an end, it's good to be aware that the animals will also begin experiencing a shortage of certain edibles. Bears will be packing in as many calories as they can, and you might find them doing so in some of the biggest remaining patches of seasonal foods, like hazelnuts. Please don't chase them away: let them have their fill and try again the next day. You might want to carry a bear horn or firearm in case you need to scare off a bear. I am careful to make my presence known while I'm out in the woods, and I've never come across a bear face-to-face. Dress in layers, and always let someone know where you will be going. You don't want to be lost out in freezing temperatures overnight.

A good digging knife can be of use for gathering burdock root and wild potato, aka groundnut (*Apios americana*), both of which are delicious fall foods.

## Common Wild Fall Foods of Minnesota
### Mitigominan—Acorns

Acorns are full of protein, carbohydrates, fats, vitamins and minerals, as well as starch and fiber. The tannic water from the leaching process is used by some to help with inflammatory ailments of the skin, and studies have shown that acorns have antibacterial, antioxidant, and gastroprotective benefits, and might even have antidiabetic properties. Where I live, there are two main types of acorns—red and white—that can be processed into flour. One requires more leaching than the other, so I've heard, but I've never made the flour from start to finish so I won't discuss that here. I have, however, had the pleasure of cooking with acorn flour, and I absolutely love the nutty, rich, roasted flavor and highly recommend you learn about acorn processing or search for an acorn flour producer near you.

### Bagaanag—Hazelnuts

Hazelnuts are a nutrient-dense food. They are a good source of manganese and vitamin E. They also contain vitamin B6, magnesium, calcium, omega fatty acids, and fiber and may help reduce blood sugar levels. Bagaanag can be harvested as early as mid- to late summer but can persist on bushes well into winter and be harvested anytime after they have ripened—if they are not first eaten by bears, squirrels, chipmunks, foxes, and larger birds like woodpeckers and turkeys. Try cooked wild rice with toasted, crushed hazelnuts and a little

Acorns

Ripe hazelnuts on the bush

Bagaanag are very beautiful.

Bagaanag that have cured for a while. Dry hazelnuts outside on a tarp or in a basket, to allow all of the grubs to come out of the nuts and wriggle away. You don't want to find them all over your house—trust me.

Bagaanag come in different sizes.

The husks come off more easily after the hazelnuts have dried.

# Ricing as a Kid and Rice Worms

**Wendy Savage, Minnesota Chippewa Nation, Lake Superior Band, Fond du Lac Reservation**

When I was young, my parents always wild riced, and it was much different than it is today. They'd go up there and there'd be all kinds of little kids all over the shore. And they would leave the kids on the shore while the parents went out ricing, but we were always told that we had to behave, we couldn't fight, and we had to be quiet while they were out on the lake. And so there'd be all these little kids on the shore, watching their parents leave in their canoes, and they'd just be kinda forlorn ... all of a sudden [the parents] would disappear into these big stalks of rice, and then you'd sit there and you'd look around, and then the kids would play, and we'd be so anxious until they would come back, and they would come back in for their lunch breaks. And it was always exciting when they came back in because we were just so happy to have our parents come back, eating, probably, cold sandwiches [laughs] on the shore.

And then other times that I went, when you'd see older people there and they'd come and they'd be cleaning their boats, they'd be picking out those wild rice worms, and there'd be one old lady that would start a little tiny fire going, and they'd be toasting and popping those wild rice worms and eating those, and they taste just like wild rice. That was another fun memory, going, "What's that little old lady doing there, making a fire there in a little tin can?"

maple sugar and salt stirred in for a tasty, healthy side dish bursting with flavor.

### Wiinisiibagoon—Wintergreen

Wintergreen contains compounds that have an effect on the body similar to aspirin. This delightfully aromatic tea is useful for the relief of muscle aches and pains, menstrual cramps, and headaches. Wiinisiibagoon treats digestive ailments like stomachache and gas. If you are pregnant or nursing, ask your plant person or doctor if wintergreen tea is okay for you. In any case, enlist a plant person to help you learn how to best make the tea for your personal use. Both the red fruits and the evergreen leaves of the wintergreen plant can be used to make tea. Wintergreen is a slow-growing plant; thus, wintergreen oil is now mostly made synthetically for use in things like toothpaste, candy, and gum. Take care to not pick too much, and only where it grows in abundance. Wintergreen can often be found growing with blueberry and bearberry plants and can be picked just about any time.

### Aniibiiminan—Highbush Cranberries

Highbush cranberries are full of vitamins A and C as well as fiber and antioxidants, and they may enhance blood glucose utilization and lipid metabolism. Aniibiiminan are not true cranberries, like those found in a mashkiig (swamp or bog). I've been told that the red fruits should be gathered after the first frost for a better taste. Some say highbush cranberries give off a "musty" odor when cooking, but jellies, jams, and syrups made with them are delicious and tangy. I am delighted to see the red fruit clinging to the ends of branches in the deep white winter and into the spring. By spring, if there are any fruit left, they are fairly dehydrated but still hold color.

Wintergreen with fruit

Aniibiiminan. *Photo by Ivy Vainio*

## Journey of Bodies

No matter where we were in the United States, when it came time for manoominike we would head home to Minnesota. My dad taught me this. Following the manoomin is one of the movements within my father that I have always recognized as essential to his character and well-being. When it comes time to harvest the manoomin, manoominike is more important to him than any other job.

# *Manoominike* Harvesting Manoomin

Akawe gidasemaakemin. Before manoominike, everyone offers tobacco. *Photo by Ivy Vainio*

Asemaa

You never know who you'll run into at the landing. Here is Ogimaagiizhig (Giniw Charwood), Nizhoo anang (Gary Charwood Sr.), Makoons (Walter Charwood), and Marvin Rogers.

Mino-giizhigad gii-manoominikeyaang. It was a beautiful day when we harvested manoomin. My first manoomin adventure ever.

Sometimes the manoomin will look so nice and thick and tall, until you get closer and see that it is growing on a floating plant mat, which is hard to near impossible to navigate. The first time I went ricing, my partner and I ended up getting stuck in these vegetative mats numerous times, and at the end of the day we had a whole thirteen pounds of manoomin! We had done much more of being stuck than we'd done ricing that day. It was still a wonderful experience, and I learned a lot. After we weighed our bag, I remembered my dad telling me that he and his cousin had gotten twelve pounds on their first time out. That made me smile.

Finding a rhythm to poling the canoe along the Mississippi while my partner, Erin Kelly, knocks manoomin

*My dad's determination and dedication to doing everything from start to finish made me want to learn how to do it all myself too.*

This Gichi-ziibi (Mississippi River) manoomin is taller than me.

I was told not to laugh while ricing. Not because it's bad luck or anything, but because you can get rice stuck in your throat—which I managed to do on my second day after a whole lot of laughing. What can I say? I was having a great time. I had that rice beard stuck in my throat for nearly a week. When I mentioned it to friends and family, someone told me to eat bread. Someone else told me to eat some honey. And someone else told me the same thing happened to them and they went to the doctor for it, but it ended up going away one day after their doctor visit. I'm not sure what actually got rid of it, but I was relieved to wake up one morning and it was gone.

My uncle Jason harvested alone and got more manoomin than we did.

After a long day of learning from being stuck in the floating plant mats, we pull our jiimaan (canoe) to the shore. We have thirteen pounds of manoomin.

Manoominike. *Photo by Jonathan Thunder*

Day two, ricing on a little lake instead of the river, is better for poling. The manoomin plants are shorter and there are no floating mats to get stuck on.

Just-knocked manoomin is teeming with life. All of the little round things in this picture are tiny insects clinging to the manoomin.

We bag our manoomin for transport. Almost two bags, about eighty pounds. Uncle gets more manoomin than us again.

Knockers. *Photo by Ivy Vainio*

138

The aluminum canoe fills up fast and becomes hairy.

Some people use wooden or birch bark canoes. *Image courtesy Manidoo Ogitigaan*

Naagaj—later the adventure will continue. Manoomin beds await.

# Where Food Grows on the Water

**Evelyn Bellanger**

Manoomin, wild rice, one of the most essential natural resources to the life of the Ojibwe in the Upper Midwest and neighboring Canada, is no longer as accessible as it once was. US laws and policies, tourism, and dam construction have changed many Ojibwe cultural practices.

Wild rice has historically been a traditional food supply for the Ojibwe. During seasonal migrations to the rice beds in August and September to harvest the crop, entire families set up camps along the shores of lakes and rivers. These camps ensured proximity to the crop and the capacity to process it, which was important to prevent it from spoiling. Mold would form if moisture was left in the rice, so processing began as soon as the harvest was unloaded from the boats. Drying, parching, hulling, and fanning the rice ensured a food supply for the coming months.

Although harvesting and processing wild rice was hard work, many Ojibwe families looked forward to it as a time of socializing. Traditionally a wild rice camp consisted of two to five or more extended families living in temporary wigwams. Sometimes fifteen to twenty families would set up an encampment on a rice lake. All shared in the communal tasks of harvesting and processing. The social life at encampments consisted of hunting, visiting, feasting, joking, horseplay, games, storytelling, romance, dancing, and exchanging news.

The traditional food supply and seasonal encampments declined as the land base was ceded through treaties and as reservation boundaries limited the Ojibwe people's freedom and land on which to harvest wild rice. Treaties excluded the Ojibwe from many of their former ricing waters; additionally, the Dawes Act of 1887 resulted in a large percentage of allotments falling into non-Native hands. The Ojibwe people encountered fences and "no trespassing" signs that prohibited them from reaching what once were places to harvest wild rice.

Most non-Natives who owned land along lakes off reservation lands restricted access to lakefronts and forbade Ojibwe people from setting up rice camps. Some required a payment of rice or cash for privileges to rice. Other lakeshore lots became resort areas, summer cabins where non-Natives enjoyed boating and fishing. The increase in motor boat traffic for sport fishing also created water wakes and pollution from gasoline, both of which affected the wild rice. Some white owners weeded out the plants to discourage Native people from ricing.

Wild rice is a relatively delicate plant. As a result of attack or damage from the elements or human intrusions, the crop can easily fail or be destroyed at any stage of growth. Wild rice is dependent on the circulation of mineral-rich water and does not tolerate chemical pollutants. Tests in Minnesota have shown the plant grows within the state's alkalinity range of 5–250 parts per million (ppm) but that it is adversely affected by sulfates and will not grow at all in water with a sulfate content of 50 ppm. It grows best in carbonate waters with a total alkalinity exceeding 40 ppm.

> "When it comes to processing rice, I take it the whole way. I start by making my stuff before ricing season starts. And then I'll harvest it, and then we process it from beginning to end. There's a lot of hard, dusty work to it. The ricing's the easy part, I think. You know, it's the work afterward that gets a little harder."
>
> — Kevin Hart Jr.

The plant anchors in soft mud with only a few short, spongy roots at its base; thus, a sudden rise in water level above six inches in June during leaf stage will uproot it. Wild rice is an annual plant that requires reseeding, and an imbalance of growth-regulatory hormones may keep it dormant for years. About half of the seeds sprout each year. Proper water levels and slow-circulating water flow are crucial factors to its growth.

Problems began when lumbering interests built coffer dams so that logs could be floated down streams to mills. The US Army Corps of Engineers undertook water-control projects that confiscated Native land for agricultural and commercial development. These projects included drainage efforts that destroyed rice beds to make room for farms and building sites, changing the courses of waterways to aid in land development, widening and channeling streambeds, and constructing locks and dams to reduce flood damage to communities along the Mississippi River. These activities destroyed wild rice habitats.

At one time wild rice beds were so vast and grew so thickly that passage through them was difficult; Natives cut passageways through the rice beds for their bark canoes. The future of natural wild rice beds is uncertain. It takes seven years for wild rice to mature. As water levels shrink due to population pressure, conversion of land to farming, and industrial growth, these plus changes in water quality yield smaller crops.

Sources consulted:

Meyer, Melissa L. *The White Earth Tragedy: Ethnicity and Dispossession at a Minnesota Anishinaabe Reservation, 1889–1920.* Lincoln and London: University of Nebraska Press, 1994.

Vennum, Thomas Jr. *Wild Rice and the Ojibway People.* St. Paul: Minnesota Historical Society Press, 1988.

*Evelyn Bellanger, of Pine Point, Minnesota, is a member of the White Earth Ojibwe Nation. She has a master's degree in American Indian studies and is a member of the Rights of Manoomin. She is a historical trauma presenter, serves on the Elders Indian Affairs Commission, and writes educational articles for the tribal newspaper* Anishinaabeg Today. *Evelyn is currently writing a memoir.*

*I met Evelyn in a writer's cohort based out of Minneapolis in 2020. I learned she has contributed to establishing the Rights of Manoomin, which is an ordinance modeled after the Rights of Nature and was passed in December 2018 by the 1855 Treaty Authority (East Lake, Leech Lake, Mille Lacs, Sandy Lake, and White Earth bands of Ojibwe). The Rights of Manoomin recognizes manoomin is "a gift from the Creator or Great Spirit and ... possesses inherent rights to exist, flourish, regenerate, and evolve, as well as inherent rights to restoration, recovery, and preservation."*

"Me and my partner have taken two to three bags of rice up to the elementary school, where we finish it throughout the day. We'd get to show them and explain to them what they were doing. That was pretty interesting. We did that for about four to five years. It was always a good experience. The little ones are always willing to learn or sit and watch and ask questions. They're always full of questions, you know. It's nice. And teachers who are always full of questions. That was good."
— Kevin Hart Jr.

# Processing Manoomin

We spread out the manoomin in the sun to dry completely. This takes a few days. You have to turn it as it dries. We do this while harvesting continues and we get ready to parch.

We heat the kettle to nice and hot and then let it cool just slightly.

Small-scale parching camp

Parching helps to preserve the manoomin. You have to stir the manoomin during the parching process. These batches took about twelve minutes each. Manoomin is ready when it has turned golden brown and smells deliciously toasted and most of the beards have fallen off.

Annie Thunder parches manoomin.

Jonathan Thunder tries his hand at parching.

The smoke will chase you around camp.

Sometimes you need to dress for the smoke. *Photo by Jonathan Thunder*

Keep a baking sheet or manoomin tray nearby to pull the manoomin onto when it's done. Let it cool a few minutes. It's nice to have a little sweep brush to clean out the beard remnants from the kettle after each batch. We use a brush with natural fibers so it doesn't melt.

Cooled, parched manoomin is bagged until the next step: jigging—dancing on the rice.

Makizinan (moccasins) are worn to dance on the manoomin.

After several minutes, the hard outer coating starts to come off.

We parch more manoomin with the Day family, Paul, Elizabeth, and Betty, from Leech Lake.

Elizabeth Day takes a turn.

Parched and cooling manoomin, soon to be danced on

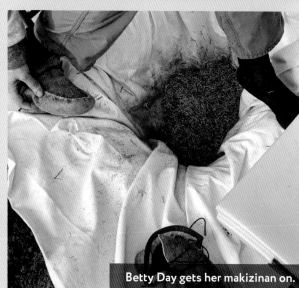
Betty Day gets her makizinan on.

Betty Day dances on the manoomin. The family dug a hole in the ground to put the manoomin in. You have to steady yourself as you dance.

Betty Day winnows manoomin for her family.

# Wild Teas with Toasted Manoomin

**VEGAN, GLUTEN FREE**                                                      Serves 1

*This recipe works for many wild dried herbal teas, like blackberry, raspberry leaf, echinacea, hyssop, and more. Try blending the leaves, flowers, fruits, and manoomin in varying proportions to find your own favorite tea blends. I suggest the total amount of ingredients equal about 1 tablespoon (3 teaspoons). This suggestion is for a blended recipe only, as described below; some individual herbal ingredients will be too strong at a full tablespoon for 8 ounces of water. If you have questions about wild herbs and any medications you might be taking, or if you are pregnant or nursing, please ask your health care provider for medical advice.*

*Suggested combinations:*
*dried nettle, dried squash, blueberries, and manoomin*
*blackberry leaf, dried black elderberries, and manoomin*
*raspberry leaf, dried currants, and manoomin*

8–12 ounces water
1–2 teaspoons favorite wild herbal blend (dried flowers, leaves, nettles work too)
1–2 teaspoons small pieces dried fruit (crab apple, squash, berries)
1–2 teaspoons Dry-Toasted Manoomin (page 33)
sweetener of choice

Boil water, then turn off the heat. Steep herbs, fruit, and manoomin using a tea ball or cloth bag; alternatively, let it go wild and strain tea after the steeping is done. Cover and let sit 5 minutes. Strain if needed. Sweeten if desired and serve.

Assorted wildflowers and fruits for tea

Rose and forget-me-nots going into the dehydrator

Tiny, dried wild black raspberries are packed with flavor.

# Iced Manoomin-Infused Crab Apple Juice

VEGAN, GLUTEN FREE                                    Makes 4 cups

*I absolutely love the flavor of crab apple juice and anything with crab apple in it. Crab apple trees have beautiful showy flowers often accompanied by a mesmerizing floral aroma in the spring that helps wake and open the heart muscles for the rest of the season. Crab apple flowers can be dried and stored, can be incorporated into teas, and make for a stunning plating element.*

4 cups crab apple juice (see below)
2 tablespoons dried apple blossoms

4 tablespoons Dry-Toasted Manoomin (page 33)
sweetener to taste

Warm crab apple juice in a small pot over medium-low heat. Place blossoms and manoomin in a reusable cloth tea bag and let steep in warm juice for a few minutes. Cool and sweeten as desired. Serve over ice.

## Crab Apple Juice

Prepare crab apple juice as you would make apple cider. Put apples in a large pot, cover with water, and simmer until the sweet-tart flavor has been transferred to the liquid. I like to core my crab apples, but some of them can be very small and I've heard that other people toss them in the pot whole. Don't use an aluminum pot, as the acid in fruits interacts with the metal. Crab apples are more tart than regular apples, so you'll probably want to sweeten and add extra water to suit your taste.

# Manoomin Pumpkin Nog

**VEGAN, GLUTEN FREE**                                                    Serves 2

*I have always had a weakness for eggnog, but all of the dairy in traditional nog doesn't agree with me. This recipe is more in line with what my body will tolerate, and it's delicious. You can switch it up and add maple extract instead of vanilla or use a dash of powdered cayenne for some heat; the possibilities for flavor combinations are endless. That's how I like my recipes!*

2 cups Manoomin Milk (page 37)
2 tablespoons pumpkin puree
2 tablespoons maple syrup
pinch nutmeg
pinch cinnamon

pinch salt
½ teaspoon vanilla extract
Ginger Maple Sugar Manoomin
    Dust (page 122) or whipped
    topping for serving

Whisk together milk, pumpkin, maple syrup, nutmeg, cinnamon, and salt in a saucepan over medium-low heat until smooth and hot. Allow to simmer for a minute, then remove from heat and stir in vanilla. Serve hot; sprinkle with Ginger Maple Sugar Manoomin Dust or serve with whipped topping if desired.

# *Oginiig* Rosehips

Itchy *jiid* (pronounced *jeed*, like *seed*) was one of the first references to wild edible plants I learned as a kid. Or at least it was one of the most memorable, as the name was always delivered by my father or one of his friends accompanied by a snicker. We'll return to that in a minute.

Now *jiid* isn't exactly a standalone word in the Anishinaabe language, but rather is spoken in terms of "his jiid" or "her jiid" or "their jiid." So to say "itchy jiid" is kind of a slang usage. I'd never heard anyone outside of Red Lake call oginiig by this name, but it wasn't until I was an adult that I realized it must be somewhat of a localized term. It was my father who told me this name, itchy jiid, and it was my mother who told me the name rosehip. The rose is the focus of art, literature, music, festivities, food, medicine, and traditions spanning continents and millennia.

If you are familiar with rosehips, you know not to ingest the seeds, for they are covered in irritating hairs. If you happen to eat them, let's just say you can expect an itchy departure. If we kids wanted to eat the fruit, my dad would instruct us to nibble around the middle where the seeds are. I always thought rosehips were like tiny, waxy, creamy apples and loved finding them on our outdoor adventures. They are firmer before snow, mushier after.

When dried and eaten plain—which delivers a special kind of crunchiness—oginiig taste like tomatoes, but when cooked and sweetened, dried or fresh rosehips smell and taste more like apples. It's not surprising that ogin, the Anishinaabe word for a rosehip, is also our word for a tomato.

Rosehips are an excellent source of vitamins C and A as well as fiber, and they contain manganese, magnesium, calcium, potassium, iron, and other vitamins and minerals. Some people believe the rose can help revive a person from emotional numbness and depression and revitalize a desire to live in the moment. I can attest to this effect.

A few years back, I was in the process of reviving myself from exactly such a state—a process that has taken decades to date—and I found myself in the Sioux Chef kitchen in Minneapolis working with rose petals with my friend, and at the time kitchen manager, Andrea Weber. We gave the petals a bath in chilled water and added honey before putting them in a dehydrator. The smells from this entire process impressed upon me a desire to live more in charge of my own life—carpe diem, as they say. Working with the roses over those few days had an effect that I can still feel anytime I wish by remembering their smell and how beautiful their presence was. Whenever I have worked with roses since, my experience has been the same. It's almost as if they are the essence of love itself, which when you're in need of self-love can be a powerfully moving and uplifting force. I find much gratitude working with plants, and the rose has a special, integrated role in my plant-memory repository.

Oginiig on the bush. Notice the compound leaves.

Dried wild oginiig

Adding maple sugar

Remove the seeds.

# Rose Sauce

**VEGAN, GLUTEN FREE**                    Makes about 1 cup

*This sauce has a potent rose flavor and can be incorporated into many recipes. Try it as a marinade for grilled meats and veggies, as a salad dressing, with sparkling water for a wild-rose soda, spilled on pancakes, blended with other fruit sauces—the possibilities are endless. Have fun exploring!*

*Rosehips and petals can be wild harvested, cultivated, and purchased at some local health food or herbal stores. For more ways to incorporate rose into your diet, search for how to make popular food and medicinal preparations like tea, syrup, jelly, and seed oil.*

1½ cups water
½ cup rosehips, seeds removed
¼–½ cup maple sugar
1 cup rose water (see sidebar)

In a small saucepan, bring water and rosehips to a boil. Reduce heat to medium-low, cover, and simmer until the rosehips begin to soften, about 8 minutes. Increase heat to medium and simmer, uncovered, 5 minutes more. Stir, then add ¼ cup maple sugar and stir again. Allow mixture to simmer on low, stirring occasionally, until sauce thickens and fruit bits are quite soft, 20–30 minutes. Remove from heat. Whisk until sauce is as smooth as you can make it. Allow to cool slightly.

Next, either blend sauce in a food processor or strain out the bits using a fine mesh strainer. If you blend it, you will have a little more fiber in your sauce. It's delicious either way.

After blending or straining the sauce, whisk in rose water and up to another ¼ cup of maple sugar, to taste. The sauce should have a color and consistency similar to that of barbecue sauce.

# Rose Water

Bring 1 cup water to boiling. Remove from heat, stir in ½ cup rose petals, and cover. Let sit at least 5 minutes. Stir, cover, and let sit another 5 minutes. Petals should be a much lighter shade and water should be a rose color. Strain.

Fresh wild roses

Dried wild roses. If using a dehydrator, be sure to use a very low setting.

# Sweet Potato Corn Pudding with Rose Sauce

VEGAN, GLUTEN FREE                                               Serves 3–5

3 cups water
2 teaspoons salt
1 cup cornmeal
1 cup mashed sweet potato (or
   substitute pumpkin, applesauce,
   or mashed bananas)

½ cup cooked manoomin
maple syrup or sugar to taste
Rose Sauce (page 153)
berries for serving

Place water and salt in a medium or large pot and bring to a boil. Reduce to medium heat and slowly whisk in cornmeal, stirring constantly until mixture is smooth. Simmer about 7 minutes (or follow instructions per type of cornmeal used). Whisk in sweet potato. Stir in manoomin. Add sweetener to taste. Serve with Rose Sauce and berries.

> **TIP:** This mix, sans rose sauce, can also be chilled and made into patties or cut into half-inch-thick pieces; fry them in a pan with a little oil or butter.

Wild Rice–Stuffed Squash. *Image courtesy Marisa Lee*

Wild Rice–Stuffed Squash. *Image courtesy Marisa Lee*

*Marisa Lee (see bio page 109)*

# Wild Rice–Stuffed Squash

VEGETARIAN                                                    Serves 6–10

*This hearty vegetarian dish is perfect for chilly days. Do all the work a day or two ahead and heat the dish in the oven when needed.*

3–4 winter squash
4 tablespoons butter
1 onion, chopped
1 celery heart, chopped
3–4 fresh sage leaves, chopped
1 teaspoon salt

2 cups wild rice
4 cups broth
2 cups water
1 cup chopped pecans
1 cup dried sour cherries

Heat oven to 400 degrees. Cut squash in half lengthwise and remove seeds. Place cut side down on baking sheets and roast in oven until tender, about 40 minutes. Set aside to cool.

In a large pot, melt butter, then add onions, celery, sage, and salt and cook, stirring often. When onions become translucent, add wild rice, broth, and water, and bring to a boil. Reduce heat and simmer, covered, for 30 minutes. Drain any excess liquid. Stir in pecans and cherries.

Once squash has cooled enough to handle, scoop out additional flesh to form a channel for stuffing, leaving ½ inch of flesh in place. Fill both halves of each squash with stuffing and place cut sides together. Tie with kitchen string if desired.

Arrange stuffed squash in a baking dish, surrounding them with excess squash and remaining stuffing, if desired. Just before serving, reheat at 350 degrees for 25–30 minutes. Slice into half moons to serve.

*Awanigiizhik Bruce, Turtle Mountain Band of*
*Chippewa Indians of North Dakota (see bio page 115)*

# Wild Rice–Stuffed Pumpkin

Serves 8–10

*Boozhoo gakina awiya! Welcome everyone! This recipe was made as a decolonized version of a Thanksgiving meal. I wanted to utilize savory, sweet, and hardy flavor profiles. Creativity as an artist translates to my expression as an experimental cook. I love to make my dishes more Ojibwe. This meal is versatile. You can substitute ingredients and make it your own flavor profile. Please enjoy and make this recipe a family favorite from mine to yours.*

3 cups wild rice
1 green bell pepper, chopped
4 radishes, chopped
2 ribs celery, chopped
1 red onion, chopped
2 carrots, peeled and sliced
4 slices smoked bacon, chopped
1 medium pumpkin
butter
⅔ cup dried tart cherries, rehydrated in hot water, then drained

¼ cup dried maitake mushrooms, rehydrated in hot water, then drained
8 cups broth
splash marsala wine
splash soy sauce
thyme
sage
Chinese five-spice powder
cumin
salt
brown sugar

Heat oven to 350 degrees.

Bring 6 cups of water to a boil. Add the wild rice. Reduce heat; cover and simmer for 30–45 minutes, depending on the type of wild rice. Drain and set rice aside to cool.

Add peppers, radishes, celery, onions, carrots, and bacon to a skillet and cook, stirring often, until vegetables are soft and bacon is crispy.

Cut open pumpkin at top near the stem, as if it is a cooking vessel with a cover; remove seeds. Coat the interior of the pumpkin with a generous amount of butter. Fill the pumpkin with the cooked vegetables and bacon, plus cherries, mushrooms, broth, wine, and seasonings to taste. Set the pumpkin into a pan. Bake for 1 hour 30 minutes or until the pumpkin is fully cooked. Enjoy your meal.

Miigwech sa dago mii'iw! Thank you and that's all!

# Maple Manoomin Patties with Tea-Infused Squash and Maple Rosehips

Serves 2–4

*This sweet version of manoomin patties makes a lovely fall appetizer or sweet and savory dessert. Follow the basic directions for Nutty Manoomin Patties but leave out the mushrooms and leeks. Instead, add a little maple sugar to sweeten the dough. Try it served with caramel drizzle (page 201).*

1 butternut squash, halved and
    seeded (see sidebar page 173)
sunflower oil
½ cup condensed tea (see page
    64; I used swamp tea)
1 cup water

½ cup dried rosehips, seeds removed
¼ cup maple syrup
Nutty Manoomin Patties (page
    62; see note above)
garnishes such as dried flowers, optional

Heat oven to 375 degrees. Line a baking pan with parchment paper. Rub squash halves with a little sunflower oil and put face down on prepared pan. Roast until squash is soft, about 30–35 minutes. Cool. Scoop out the creamy squash into a food processor. Blend with tea to a scoopable but not runny consistency.

In a small saucepan, bring water and rosehips to a boil. Reduce heat to medium low, cover, and simmer until the rosehips begin to soften, about 8 minutes. Uncover, increase heat to medium, and simmer 5 minutes more. Stir. Add maple syrup and stir again. Reduce heat to low and simmer, stirring occasionally, until rosehip sauce thickens. Use an immersion blender to puree mixture (you might want to blend sauce in a deep container so it doesn't splatter out). Leave a little texture and shape with the rosehips; don't blend it too smooth. (Alternatively, have at it: blend it as smooth as you like!) This step can take 15–30 minutes, depending on desired smoothness.

Top manoomin patties with squash and rosehips sauce. Add any garnishes you like; dried flowers are lovely.

**Andi Murphy**

The first time I had wild rice was in the office break room.

Monica, my coworker and good friend, brought out a large plastic Tupperware filled with a greasy mess of brown and gray wild rice dotted with cranberries and piñons. She pulled the lid off the container and scooped some rice onto her plate.

I watched. It looked interesting.

"Do you want some? It's wild rice with some cranberries and piñons. It's not very good," she said, always one to play down her cooking abilities.

"Yeah," I said.

It smelled buttery and grainy.

I observed the large, bloomed grains of rice, some looking like little curled-up brown worms. I scooped up a large spoonful and put it in my mouth (which is usually how I taste foods for the first time—with a big spoonful). Some of the grains had a small snap to them and released earthy and mushroomy flavors perfectly accentuated by the sweet cranberries and piney, roasted nuts.

"This is pretty great," I said, going in for another spoonful.

"It's from Fond du Lac," she said.

My eyebrows shot up and my eyes got big.

"Yeah, remember Mr. Savage? He told me he sold wild rice and I bought a pound," she said.

"I want some next time," I said.

"Well, we can order some pretty soon. This is the last of the rice I had," she said. "I can just call him up."

A few days later, we got a package of wild rice from Mr. Savage from the Fond du Lac reservation in Minnesota.

My first taste of Native wild rice was inspiring. From that day forward, I made sure to have a steady supply of Native wild rice in my pantry. Since then, I've bought wild rice from Red Lake and White Earth, and today's supply is from Spirit Lake Native Farms. I stuffed my luggage with seven pounds of Spirit Lake rice when I took a trip to Minnesota in September 2019.

Being from New Mexico and the Navajo Nation, I thought of wild rice as a foreign ingredient. It made appearances only in conference-style banquet meals with two other kinds of rice in pilaf. When I got ahold of the real deal, I cooked it simply. My coworker told me about the three-to-one ratio, but I quickly noticed that wild rice from different lakes took various amounts of time and liquid. They even looked different and smelled different. Some took on more of a gray color and others had a very light green tint. But each batch of wild rice I made has always been special. None of it has gone to waste.

Wild rice recently made an appearance for the first time at the Food Distribution Program on Indian Reservations, what some still call the "commodities" food program. My father works there, and he called me one day to say, "Ann [my parents and sister are the only people who call me 'Ann'], we got some wild rice at the warehouse. How do you cook it?"

Mind you, this is my very Navajo father, who had never cooked wild rice before and had been introduced to it by me just a few months prior.

"Wow!" I exclaimed, completely excited for the people in my hometown who would be getting wild rice as part of their program food packages. "Wild rice is so good. I'll make it for you next time you visit."

"We got a shipment of wild rice, and people don't know what it is. A bunch of people already refused it," he said.

My heart sank. Of course people in my hometown reservation are not familiar with wild rice. Crownpoint, New Mexico, is nearly 1,500 miles from the Great Lakes. This is the desert Southwest. We eat a lot of corn, beans, squash, mutton, and chile. Nothing close to wild rice.

I gave my dad directions to that wild rice, cranberry,

and piñon dish I fell in love with. "It's pretty simple. If they can make that, I think they'll be hooked."

And then I got an idea to make short cooking videos. Visual directions make more sense than some program director or nutritionist talking at people and telling them how they should cook and eat something. At least, that's how I always felt about food and food conversations.

Before we hung up, I said, "Wait, I have an idea!"

My dad said, "What?"

"Have you seen some of those Tasty videos? They're like thirty seconds to a minute and it's shot from the top?"

"Yeah," he said, but I knew he had no idea because he's not on social media. My mom shows him a lot of things on Facebook by leaning over and sharing her phone.

"How about I make a short video like that on wild rice? It'll be short and simple."

Of course, the photographer in me was thinking about the light set up, the camera rig, what materials need to be purchased to make such a rig, and how I'm going to edit this video on my ancient desktop computer.

"I think people would be more inspired to cook this wild rice—do you know how precious wild rice is?—if they saw it in a short, well-made video. We need some kind of tripod that holds the camera directly above the burner."

"I can make it," he chimed in.

"Yes! We just have to find a little mount piece that goes directly into my camera."

And so we were on a mission, my dad and I.

We shared DIY YouTube videos and had multiple conversations about the construction of the studio. I ordered ridiculously bright lights online, and we got to work making a little video studio box that fit on a big table I had sitting in my garage.

My dad loves projects like these, and it's great to have his support in any building project endeavor. I don't

Image courtesy Andi Murphy

think he really knew what part he was playing in this Native food movement.

The biggest part of the movement, I think, is sharing. We share a lot.

*Andi Murphy (Diné) is the creator, host, and producer of the* Toasted Sister Podcast, *a show about Indigenous food. A freelance food writer and speaker, she's also a producer with* Native America Calling, *a one-hour national radio show about Indigenous issues and topics. Andi grew up on the Navajo reservation in New Mexico. She has a journalism degree from New Mexico State University and has been working as a journalist since 2011. She's also a photographer, a home cook, and an amateur artist who creates all the art for the* Toasted Sister Podcast. *She lives in Albuquerque, New Mexico, with her cats, Carrot and Lucifur.*

*I've known Andi for a few years now thanks to our mutual multimedia interests. I'm honored to have her share her story about manoomin and excited for you all to try her delicious recipe. To learn more about her work, visit www.toastedsisterpodcast.com.*

**Andi Murphy**

# Bison and Wild Rice–Stuffed Poblano Pepper with Pumpkin Seed Sauce

GLUTEN FREE                                                      Makes 4–5 stuffed chiles

*I like this recipe because the ingredients really speak for themselves. There isn't a long list of spices or intricate cooking techniques involved, just some good knife work.*

4–5 poblano peppers
oil
1 pound ground bison
salt
1 small to medium onion, diced
1 small to medium tomato, diced
1 small to medium apple, diced
½ cup dried cranberries, rehydrated in
    hot water for 5 minutes, then drained
1½ cups diced squash (butternut
    or acorn) or pumpkin

2 tablespoons maple syrup
1½ cups cooked wild rice
¼ cup toasted pine nuts
1½ cup toasted pumpkin seeds
1 cup cashew milk
2 teaspoons agave syrup
1 tablespoon amaranth flour
    (or local nut flour)
seeds of 1 pomegranate for topping,
    optional (see tip page 95)

Over an open flame (outside or on your kitchen stove), roast peppers until skin blisters and turns black. Put peppers in a plastic bag and let them sweat for about 10 minutes. (This loosens the skin and makes it easier to peel.) Peel peppers, then make a single, long slit down the length of the pepper and clean out the seeds.

In a large skillet heat a teaspoon or two of oil and cook bison seasoned with salt, stirring, until browned. Add onions and cook until translucent. Add tomatoes and apples, and cook until apples are soft. Stir in cranberries.

In a separate, small skillet, cook squash, stirring, for about 5 minutes, until tender. Add maple syrup and let syrup caramelize around squash. Add to the bison mixture. Mix in wild rice and pine nuts.

Add pumpkin seeds, cashew milk, agave, and amaranth flour to a blender, and blend until smooth and light green. Add a little more cashew milk to thin as necessary.

Stuff each poblano pepper with one-quarter or one-fifth of the bison mixture. Ladle on the sauce and garnish with pomegranate seeds.

Bison and Wild Rice–Stuffed Poblano Pepper with Pumpkin Seed Sauce. *Image courtesy Andi Murphy*

*Photo by Cara Totman Photography*

*Kristina Stanley (Ojibwe) is an activist, chef, and community organization consultant currently located in south-central Wisconsin. As a student of ecopsychology, she has dedicated her life to deepening her understanding of food ecosystems, food access, and how our individual and communal relationships with food and the natural environment impact both physical and mental health. She currently serves the community as a program manager with the I-Collective and as the food and culinary program coordinator with Native American Food Sovereignty Alliance (NAFSA).*

*Kristina Stanley*

# Juniper-Brined Turkey with Wild Rice–Cornbread Stuffing

Serves 10–12

*This recipe is perfect for large families or family gatherings. Each component is packed with flavor. If you've never harvested juniper berries before, this brining technique is the perfect reason to do so.*

1 (10- to 30-pound) turkey

## For the brine

⅔ cup salt
⅔ cup maple syrup
2 tablespoons crushed juniper berries
2 teaspoons crushed
   black peppercorn

2 tablespoons crushed allspice berries
5–6 leaves fresh garden sage
2–3 bay leaves
8 cups hot water
4 cups ice water

## For the cornbread

1¾ cups + 2 tablespoons sunflower oil
5½ cups sweet corn
1 cup unsweetened almond milk
¾ cup maple syrup
3 eggs
1½ cups cassava flour

¼ cup cornstarch
1⅓ cups cornmeal
1½ teaspoons salt
1 teaspoon baking powder
½ teaspoon baking soda

## For roasting

1 large onion, chopped
3 cloves garlic, sliced
7 leaves fresh garden sage
sunflower oil

salt and pepper
powdered sumac
smoked paprika

## For the dressing

½ cup caramelized onion (see tip)
2 cups sweet corn
2 tablespoons minced fresh sage
   + whole leaves for garnish
4 eggs
1 cup stock (use turkey drippings
   mixed with veggie/chicken/
   or turkey stock)

1 cup almond milk
2 teaspoons salt
1 teaspoon pepper
3 cups cooked wild rice
sunflower oil for drizzling

In a large pot, combine brine ingredients except ice water. Bring to a boil for a few minutes, then add to ice water. Immerse turkey and soak, rotating once in a while, 12–24 hours. Then drain, rinse, pat dry, and let stand, uncovered, in refrigerator 6 hours or overnight.

To make the cornbread, heat oven to 375 degrees and grease a 10x12–inch baking dish. Heat 1¾ cups oil in a deep pot. Add corn and cook until golden, then blend with immersion blender. Add milk and maple syrup and blend again; add eggs and blend again. Stir in flour, cornstarch, cornmeal, salt, baking powder, and baking soda. Spread batter into prepared pan and bake until internal temperature reaches 194 degrees, about 35–45 minutes. Cool, then crumble for the dressing.

To roast the turkey, fill turkey cavity with onion, garlic, and sage and rub outside with oil mixed with salt and pepper, sumac, and paprika. Place turkey in a roasting pan on a rack set over enough water to coat bottom of pan. Roast at 500 degrees just until skin begins to brown/crisp, then reduce heat to 350 degrees. Baste frequently and cook until internal temperature is 165 degrees (approximately 15 minutes per pound of turkey). Reserve drippings for dressing. Let turkey rest at least 45 minutes before cutting or serving.

To make the dressing, heat oven to 375 degrees and grease a large (12x20–inch) baking dish. Mix together crumbled cornbread, onion, corn, minced sage, eggs, stock, milk, salt, and pepper. Mix thoroughly, then fold in wild rice. Pour into prepared pan, arrange sage leaves over top, drizzle with oil, and sprinkle with salt. Bake for 30–45 minutes. Serve with turkey.

> **TIP:** I usually put salt and a sage leaf or two in with the onions as they caramelize, and I also like to add the corn at this stage.

# Manoomin Gravy

Serves 2–4

hot cooked manoomin
vegetable broth or bone stock
salt and pepper

pinch garlic powder, optional
1 tablespoon roasted leeks, optional

Put a couple cups of hot cooked manoomin into a blender, add broth or stock in ¼ cup increments, and blend until gravy reaches desired thickness. Season with salt and pepper to taste. A pinch of garlic powder or a tablespoon of roasted leeks is good at this point too, if you like a garlicky gravy, like I do. Blend smooth and serve hot over anything in need of a good smothering of gravy.

*Photo by Joseph Erb*

*Melissa E. Lewis is a citizen of Cherokee Nation and lives in Tahlequah, Oklahoma, with her husband and son. Among many other activities, Melissa hosts classes in her community to teach about traditional foods, culture, language, and nutrition. I am honored to be able to share her recipe featuring her people's wild traditional foods alongside manoomin.*

*Melissa E. Lewis*

# ᎤᏍᏗ, ᏔᏟᏍᎦ ᎡᎳ ᎥᏓᎩ, ᎠᏓ ᏟᎮᏴᎦ ᏍᏍ ᏟᎮᏓᎣᎪᏗ

## *Persimmon, Wild Rice, and Chinquapin Donuts*

Makes 12 donuts

*Adapted from Persimmon Cake by Kristin Rosenau,* The Pastry Affair, *and Persimmon Cake Donuts by Ruby Josephine*

¾ cup persimmon puree (see tip)
1 cup granulated sugar (or substitute other sweeteners like maple sugar)
½ cup oil (vegetable, olive, coconut, avocado)
2 small chicken eggs or 1 large duck egg or 8 quail eggs, beaten
1 teaspoon vanilla extract
¼ cup nut milk
½ cup wild rice flour (page 35)
1½ cups flour (all-purpose, gluten free)

2 teaspoons baking powder
½ teaspoon ground cinnamon
½ teaspoon ground nutmeg
½ teaspoon ground cardamom
½ teaspoon ground ginger
½ teaspoon salt
½ cup chopped chinquapin + more for sprinkling
powdered sugar, cinnamon sugar, or frosting for topping

Heat oven to 350 degrees and grease donut pan.

In a large bowl, stir together persimmon puree, sugar, oil, eggs, vanilla, and milk. In another bowl, mix together flours, baking powder, spices, and salt. Stir dry ingredients into wet ingredients until the mixture is smooth and there are no lumps. Stir in chinquapins.

Carefully pour or spoon the batter into individual molds in the prepared pan, filling up about three-quarters of the mold with batter and smoothing the top. Bake until a tester inserted into donut comes out clean, about 12–15 minutes.

Either sprinkle lightly with powdered sugar or cinnamon sugar or add your favorite frosting before serving. Sprinkle additional chinquapins on top of each donut.

Fall is a beautiful time for fruits and nuts. In Cherokee Nation, after the frost persimmons fall from trees and are about the sweetest gift you have ever tasted from nature. They also are weather predictors: if you split open the seed and you see a spoon that means you will be shoveling snow, but if you see a knife it means it will be cold and cutting. A fork means the winter will be mild. Chinquapins and other nuts are ready to harvest at this time as well. Persimmons and chinquapins both have some unique challenges to successful eating; one is full of seeds and the other is quite prickly, so a colander and gloves are a must. Wild rice flour adds a nice earthy flavor to the sweetness of persimmon and chinquapins. Definitely pair with apple cider and other delicious, aromatic fall foods.

**TIP:** I prefer foraging for local persimmon, but any kind of persimmon can be used. Persimmons native to the United States have quite a few seeds. To make the puree, use a colander to extract the pulp from the seeds, which can be a time-consuming job. Return the seeds back to the tree for the animals to do their work of efficient seed spreading.

Photo by Christina Winkle

Nico Albert is a citizen of the Cherokee Nation (ᏣᎳᎩ ᎠᏰᎵ), descended from the Adair family originating in the Cherokee lands now known as Georgia. Her journey to learn traditional Cherokee ways and dishes and the wild and cultivated ingredients involved in their preparation grew to encompass the indigenous cuisines of tribes from all parts of North America and sparked a passion for Indigenous food revitalization and food sovereignty. She is the founder and executive chef of Burning Cedar Indigenous Foods, a catering and consulting company specializing in traditional and modern Native American foods. Nico lives on the Mvskoke (Creek) reservation (otherwise known as Tulsa, Oklahoma) with her husband Kyle (Ponka/Otoe-Missouria/Iowa), stepdaughter Khloe, two mischievous dogs, and three perfect rabbits. Nico and her family enjoy traveling, spending time outdoors in their garden and near water, and dancing at powwows.

**Nico Albert, Cherokee Nation, founder/executive chef, Burning Cedar Indigenous Foods**

# Pumpkin Walnut Manoomin Cookies

VEGETARIAN                                     Makes about 3 dozen cookies

1 cup all-purpose flour
3 cups cooked manoomin
1 teaspoon baking powder
½ teaspoon baking soda
½ teaspoon kosher salt
1 teaspoon ground cinnamon
½ teaspoon ground ginger
¼ teaspoon ground nutmeg
⅛ teaspoon ground cloves

2 tablespoons coconut oil, at room temperature
½ cup granulated sugar
½ cup loosely packed brown sugar
1 egg
6 tablespoons pumpkin puree or other winter squash puree
2 teaspoons vanilla extract
1 cup chopped walnuts

Heat oven to 350 degrees and line 2 baking sheets with parchment paper.

In a medium bowl, whisk together flour, manoomin, baking powder, baking soda, salt, and spices.

In a large bowl, combine the coconut oil, sugars, egg, pumpkin, and vanilla. Use a hand mixer on medium speed to mix well. Add the dry ingredients to the sugar mixture. Stir all the ingredients together by hand until just combined with no streaks of flour remaining, then stir in the walnuts.

Drop tablespoon portions onto prepared baking sheets. Bake for about 10–15 minutes, until cookies are light brown at the edges. Cool on baking sheet for 3–4 minutes, then transfer to a wire rack to cool completely.

# Toasted Manoomin and Bagaan (Hazelnut) Butter Chocolate Cups

*Get adventurous with this recipe! Try a variety of types of chocolate, add dried fruit, flowers, whole or halved nuts, caramel—whatever you want.*

mini muffin tin or candy mold
1½ cups chopped semisweet
   chocolate, chips, or other favorite
   chocolate, melted until smooth

Dry-Toasted Manoomin (page
   33, or use any another
   popped manoomin method)
½ cup Bagaan (Hazelnut)
   Butter (page 171)
sea salt, optional

If using a metal pan, line with paper liners. Use two spoons to scoop about 1 teaspoon of melted chocolate into each cup, then use the back of a spoon to smear the chocolate to coat the sides of each cup. Sprinkle in toasted manoomin, as much as you want. Add about ½ to 1 teaspoon Bagaan Butter, leaving room to cover with more chocolate. Add about 1 more teaspoon of chocolate on top. Use spoon or butter knife to smooth out the tops. Sprinkle with a little sea salt if desired. Let chocolates cool and harden before serving.

Toasted Manoomin and Bagaan Butter Chocolate Cups

Swirl the chocolate on the sides of the cups.

Sprinkle in toasted manoomin and add a dab of bagaan butter.

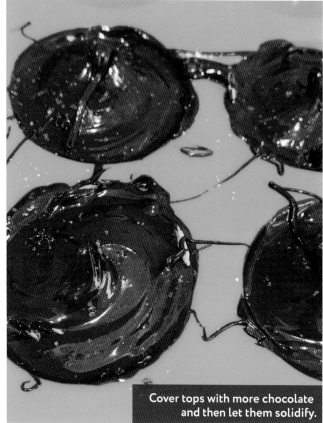

Cover tops with more chocolate and then let them solidify.

Pay close attention when toasting so that bagaanag do not get too brown.

Rub the warm bagaanag with a clean dish towel.

Removing the skins will make the butter a little less bitter.

Roasted bagaanag ready to be made into butter

# Bagaan (Hazelnut) Butter

Makes about 1¾ cups

2 cups shelled roasted bagaanag (see tip)
¼ cup honey
½ teaspoon salt
3 tablespoons water (see note)

Put roasted bagaanag, honey, and salt in a very strong blender and blend to desired smoothness. This will take some time, and you will have to stop the machine to scrape down the sides. Add up to 3 tablespoons water for a chunky texture (see note).

> **TIP:** Spread raw bagaanag (hazelnuts), shelled or not, in a single layer on a baking sheet and roast at 300 degrees for 10–12 minutes, until they smell toasty. Shelled nuts are easier to gauge for doneness: they will show a little browning. If you leave the shells on, watch closely so the nuts don't burn. Remove some of the skins, which can be bitter, by pouring cooled, shelled nuts into a pot and using a cotton cloth to squeeze them together in your fist (see page 170). (Personally, I leave the skins on.)

Some blenders are capable of making roasted nut and seed butters with no extra oil or water. Mine is a middle-of-the-line blender and requires a little help to smooth out the butter. Water works fine for this recipe. If you use water in your bagaan butter, I recommend storing the chocolates in an airtight container in the fridge—if they last longer than the same day you make them, that is.

# Chokecherry Jam Cakes

VEGETARIAN                                                    Makes 6 cakes

*The cake's texture becomes less spongy as it cools.*

½ cup cassava flour or all-purpose
    flour of choice
½ cup Manoomin Flour (page 35)
⅓ cup loosely packed maple
    sugar + more for sprinkling
½ teaspoon baking powder

½ teaspoon salt
1 egg
2 tablespoons oil
⅓ cup + 2 tablespoons milk of choice
chokecherry jam

Heat oven to 350 degrees. Grease muffin pan (or leave ungreased if silicone; see tip page 110).

In a large bowl, whisk together flours, maple sugar, baking powder, and salt. In a separate bowl, whisk together egg, oil, and milk. Stir wet and dry ingredients together until just combined; mixture should have the consistency of cake batter. Put about 1 tablespoon of batter into each muffin compartment. Add about a teaspoon of jam, then cover with another tablespoon of batter. Sprinkle tops with maple sugar and bake about 15 minutes, until tester comes out clean. Let cool before serving.

Chokecherries

# Powerhouse Cookies

**VEGAN, GLUTEN FREE**                    Makes about 3 dozen cookies

*These are delicious with a dab of wild jam on top.*

## For seed butter

2 cups shelled pumpkin seeds
2 cups shelled sunflower seeds
½ cup maple syrup

½ cup honey
pinch salt
½ cup water + more as needed

## For dough

1 cup diced roasted squash (gete
    okosimaan or butternut) (see below)
1 cup cooked beans (northern)
¼ cup maple syrup
½ teaspoon salt
about 1 cup finely ground
    cornmeal or corn flour

¼ cup cooked manoomin
⅓ cup dried berries (blueberries,
    cranberries)
optional: crushed hazelnuts or
    other nut, chocolate chips,
    Puffed Amaranth (page 33)

Heat oven to 350 degrees. Line a baking sheet with parchment paper and grease paper.

Place pumpkin seeds and sunflower seeds in food processor or blender. Add ½ cup maple syrup, honey, pinch of salt, and water. Pulse or blend until consistency of peanut butter, adding more water as needed. Scrape into a large bowl and set aside.

Place squash, beans, ¼ cup maple syrup, and ½ teaspoon salt in food processor and blend until smooth. Stir into seed butter and mix well. Add enough cornmeal or corn flour to make a dough with a consistency a little wetter than peanut butter. Taste and adjust for salt and sweetness preferences. (If you add honey or maple syrup, also add a little water if needed to get the right consistency.) Fold in manoomin and dried berries, as well as nuts, chocolate chips, or puffed amaranth (if using).

Drop dough by tablespoon onto prepared baking sheet. Use a greased 5x5 square of parchment paper to press cookies to half an inch thick. This batter doesn't rise or spread; how you shape the cookies at this step will determine how thick and wide they will be when done. Sprinkle tops with a few pumpkin seeds and gently press into the dough.

Bake for 10 minutes, until golden brown, turning the pan as needed.

## Roasted Squash

Heat oven to 350 degrees. Peel and dice a small squash, toss with a drizzle of oil and maple syrup and a sprinkle of salt, and bake in a lined baking pan until squash is caramelized and soft, about 30–35 minutes. Remove from oven and let cool.

# Love Bites

VEGAN, GLUTEN FREE                                                    Makes about 2 dozen

*These Love Bites are made with rose sauce, but you can substitute other fruit sauces, like wild plum with hyssop or chunky blueberry. If you're crunched for time, use your favorite premade jam to simplify the process.*

Manoomin Pie Crust mixture (page 40)
1 cup cooled Rose Sauce (page 153), sweetened to taste
fresh wild strawberries

Grease a baking sheet or line with parchment paper or silicone mat. Moisten pie crust mixture (see tip) and make small balls of dough. Place on prepared baking sheet and push your thumb into the middle to make a reservoir.

Fill dough reservoirs with rose sauce. Place one tiny wild strawberry (or slice of a larger strawberry) sideways on top of each.

For raw bites, cool pan in fridge until centers are set. For cooked bites, bake at 350 degrees until they start to brown on the edges, about 8 minutes. Cool most of the way, then cover bites to keep them soft and allow to cool completely before serving.

> **TIP:** If you plan to serve Love Bites raw, keep your dough on the drier side and, to keep them soft, add rose sauce and then let them sit, covered, for a couple of hours in the fridge before serving.

Image courtesy Manidoo Ogitigaan

# Biboong
(bih BOONG)

## WINTER

When I was in my late twenties and living in a house with multiple roommates, I once told one of them that there were times growing up when I wouldn't eat all day. He had such a look of incomprehension for the situation and told me that the whole time he was growing up he had access to a full food pantry at home, which in turn made my mind boggle. Pretty much any time we lived off of the rez, I would have food anxieties surrounding lunchtime, as most of the time I didn't eat school lunch for whatever reason.

Filling our pantries with wild and cultivated foods is empowering. Winter is a time when it's especially comforting to have a store of dry and canned goods in your pantry or cellar. Dried herbs and fruits from spring and summer come into play, along with jams, stored nuts, flours, and frozen foods, all of which can be stored in jars.

Anyone who knows me well knows I have an obsession with jars. I love the touch of the glass, the colors, shapes, and smoothness. But what I love most is their utility. My appreciation for things having utility started at the age of eight. I had lost one of my shoes between the hay bales in the barn near our house, and for some time after that I had to wear the only pair of shoes I had left: pointy-toed, shiny black dress shoes. I will never forget walking in those dress shoes up and down our long rural driveway, through the snow to and from the bus every day. To this day I will hands down choose utility over style if given the option. I am undeniably attracted to utility. In any case, winter is a great time to pull out all of your sexy jars of jams, pickled vegetables, and gems of dried foods.

## Common Wild Winter Foods of Minnesota
### Giizhikaandagoog —White Cedar Boughs— Tree of Life

White cedar leaves can be picked year-round. Harvest from the tips of the branches. In spring the youngest leaves are bright green and tender. The leaves get tougher and the color darkens as the seasons progress. White cedar is similar to red cedar, miskwaawaak, but giizhik has flattened, scalelike leaves rather than miskwaawaak's rounded ones. When making tea, tie little boughs of leaves together with string to make it easy to remove them, or simply strain out the leaves when the steeping is done. Like spruce needles, the flattened boughs of the white cedar are high in vitamin C. We have

I noticed a small, pea-sized lump in my breast last week. I was a little scared, but this discovery made my self-listening intensify. I don't know if it was my body or the cedar that was calling out, but the connection of the two is what was called for. On that first day, I chewed up a small portion of the cedar leaves I had just gathered for tea and placed the little ball of leaves directly onto the skin above the lump. It's kind of sticky so it stayed in place under my shirt. I didn't mind that some of the bits would dry and fall off down my shirt; I was being told that it was best for me to let the air get to it rather than cover it up. I changed it out with a fresh chewed cedar ball after a few hours, at least twice a day. It's been about five days now, and the lump is gone.

# Native Hot Love

**Wendy Savage, Minnesota Chippewa Nation, Lake Superior Band, Fond du Lac Reservation**

For men to give you their little precious gifts, their baskets and things that they've made, is a real great expression of Native love, it really is. Oh, you can really tell when a Native has Native hot love for you, because things [will] come [to your] home, like they give you handmade wild rice knockers that they've made. You'll come home and find frozen fish in your back porch. [*Laughs*] You'll find things like, ah, you'll get the fillet of mignon of moose. That's how you can tell that it's Native hot love.

I got snowshoes once too. Another time, I was in the hospital and another interested party went to the grocery store and asked the produce department for an empty strawberry basket. He went around and picked all of the best strawberries and brought them to me in the hospital. So that's how you can tell there's true Native love and Native hot love, and how you can tell they really love you is when they give you that most precious little gift that you need to sustain life.

stories about giizhik and her medicine and contributions to our ways of life. In addition to tasting delicious and having an uplifting, grounding aroma, cedar is used both internally and externally for a variety of ailments. I personally drink the tea when my immune system needs a boost. It's always good to ask your local plant person and/or doctor if cedar tea is okay for you and how much to drink. If you're pregnant, please ask a plant medicine person before trying any new teas; I've heard some say pregnant women should not drink this tea. Also, as with anything, don't overindulge. There are oils in cedar that can build up to a toxic effect if you drink too much too often.

## Okosimaan—Squashes

Pumpkin and squash seeds contain protein, folate, fiber, iron, calcium, and potassium. They are a good food to eat when you're out on the water ricing all day. They also contain antioxidants to boost immune function when eaten on a regular basis, and they have anti-inflammatory effects that some people use to help treat arthritis. Winter squashes last for months, providing bright, sunny nutrition on the darkest days of the year. Squashes that have less hardy skin can be cleaned and dried to be added to soups or made into flour and used in baked goods and added to soups to thicken them and boost nutritional value and flavor.

# *Mashkiigobag* Swamp Tea (the plant)

We all have our happy places that bring us wonder or mystery, places that make us feel humble, safe, loved. One of my favorite places is also the most sensory-awakening environment I have ever had the pleasure of being immersed in: the unassuming floating sphagnum moss bogs of cool, northern climates.

There is a plant that can be found living on these floating bogs that I've heard called mashkiigobag or anii-biishaaboo. As English-speaking Anishinaabeg (people), we also say "swamp tea" for both the plant and the tea.

The scientific name for mashkiigobag is *Rhododendron groenlandicum*, aka *Ledum groenlandicum*. It is more commonly known as bog Labrador tea. This plant also has names in other tribal languages as well as names those tribes use to refer to the plant in English.

This ecosystem—the floating sphagnum moss bog—was largely avoided by colonizers in North America. "Why would anyone want to go there?" is a question that resounds still today. Let me illustrate.

One summer day I was happily, quietly, carefully squishing along atop a floating bog in rural north-central Minnesota, gazing into pitcher plants, admiring orchids, and stopping to smell the swamp tea.

After an hour or so of solitude, a nice shiny vehicle pulled up alongside the bog and parked on the side of the dirt road. A woman got out, squinted at me, and began to shout, "What are you doing out there!" It came across as less a question about what I was doing and more a question about my character. "Looking at flowers!" I replied, still crouched low. She stood there for a bit, hands on hips, obviously disturbed, then shook her head and flailed her arms as she stomped back to her vehicle and then drove away.

I should mention that you must be careful if you venture out onto a floating bog. Maybe she was concerned

for me, but that's not what it felt like. I know that mooz (moose) walk on these floating plant masses and seem to do okay. To be on the safe side, go with a friend—if for no other reason than to have someone to share the delight of squishing around on ground that dips and moves like a waterbed, but is much more enjoyable.

When I feel around into my memory, this plant is there alongside my great-grandmother, my father and his siblings, and my siblings, and I look forward to one day introducing my children to this highly revered relative. I always think of and speak to this family member with love, appreciation, and reverence. That it is a plant makes no difference.

Mashkiigobagwaaboo (swamp tea the drink) contains vitamin C. It is mildly expectorant and wards off infection, helping to relieve respiratory ailments. This tea is also a diuretic (increases urine flow).

It's a delight to find this plant in the winter, as it often sits tucked halfway under the snow, looking like a miniature pine tree with its drooping twigs. The leaves are covered in soft, orange hairs that have a very pleasant floral aroma that is further released when simmered in water.

I am often appalled by other writers' descriptions for this plant and the tea it makes. I've heard it called a weed by one and its leaves referred to as "hairy armpits" (not in a "good funny" way, either) by another who also says the tea tastes terrible. I'm not sure who these people are but they must not have spent any amount of time cultivating a quality relationship with this beautiful plant relative. And they must be really bad at making tea. I always doubt someone who characterizes a plant in such a summed-up negative way. All plants have their own special gifts.

It's a traditional tea for numerous tribes. A few weeks back a new friend from a different tribe sent me a photo showing a hollowed-out squash with some liquid and food items inside. I recognized the swamp tea immediately. "Is that swamp tea?" I asked. She knew it as something else in a Pacific Northwest language. I searched for a webpage that had some clear images and descriptions of the plant and sent it to her. "Is this it?" I asked. "Oh my god! It's the same plant!" was her reply. We were both so happy to learn of the connection and joyed to know the other shared a love for the plant.

Nowadays, mining companies rip up these plants, tear off the leaves, and analyze the contents of the stems to see if there are minute particles of gold in them and thus the nearby landscape. They target the land based on the existence of mashkiigobag—for tiny amounts of gold that only a computer can detect. Sphagnum moss is taken off of the top layer for commercial purposes. These wetlands are also changed entirely when everything is removed down to the bedrock and the area filled in with gravel. Researchers assume that once the floating sphagnum moss bogs are disturbed, these medicinal wonderlands may never return.

Swamp tea is a small shrub, usually less than three feet tall. It is an evergreen, having leaves that stay green all year round, although sometimes some of the leaves will turn a rusty, red-purple in the winter. The leaves have an exquisite, strong floral smell and a dense, soft fuzz underneath that is pale in color when the leaves are young but turns reddish-brown as the leaves mature. The sides of the elliptical, smooth-edged leaves roll under. Clusters of five-petaled white flowers bloom June–August.

When I was growing up I learned to harvest swamp tea in the winter, after the bogs are frozen and thus easier to walk on, when the flowering and fruiting season is past and the fuzz on the undersides of the leaves is dark orangish-brown and very fragrant. However, I have come to understand that almost every family has their own preference for the best time to harvest. Today I know people who harvest in the spring before the flowers, some who harvest during flowering, and others in the fall.

Sometimes you just have to sit quietly and observe on a floating bog.

On close inspection, you might find tiny cranberry leaves creeping across the sphagnum moss.

Swamp tea

Swamp tea with flower buds

The undersides of swamp tea are pale and fuzzy when young, orange and fuzzy when mature. The leaves are very florally aromatic.

Swamp tea will make your entire house smell amazing.

# Mashkiigobagwaaboo (Swamp Tea)

Serves 6–8

*Swamp tea lifts away my anxieties and allows my focus to come into tune with my creativity and productiveness. It feels like a good dose of health for my whole being.*

**6 cups water**
**about 1 cup fresh or dried whole swamp tea leaves**
**honey or other sweetener to taste**

Heat water and add tea in a tea bag or ball or loose if you plan to strain later. I personally brew leaves loose as I like to watch them dance around during the simmering. Let tea simmer on low for about 20 minutes, stirring with a wooden spoon every few minutes. You will know it's ready when your house is filled with a beautiful floral aroma and the tea is yellowish in color. Strain, sweeten, and enjoy.

> **TIP:** Follow the basic tea recipe but add in a small bundle of sumac berries and/or ½ cup fruit of your choice. Or steep ½ cup Dry-Toasted Manoomin (page 33) in tea off heat after leaves are removed. Strain and sweeten.

Swamp tea can stimulate menstruation and so should not be taken by pregnant women. If you are nursing or taking medication, consult with a physician.

# Wild Manoomin Fruit Sodas

VEGAN, GLUTEN FREE                                               Serves 4

*I prefer my wild sodas mildly sweet, as in this recipe, but you might like things sweeter. Try adding a piece of fresh fruit or mint leaf for serving.*

1 cup water
4 tablespoons wild herbal blend
    (see Wild Teas with Toasted
    Manoomin, page 146)

¼ cup maple syrup, to taste
ice
3 cups sparkling water

Add water and herbal blend to a small pot. Bring to a low boil, then remove from heat, cover, and let sit for 10 minutes. Strain into a large glass measuring cup or other dish with a spout, then stir in maple syrup and allow to cool completely (also see recipe for Manoomin Smoothie, below).

Fill four 8-ounce glasses halfway with ice, then divide syrup and sparkling water among them.

## Manoomin Smoothie

I love fruit and tea in my smoothies. Blend 1–2 tablespoons chilled herbal tea blend concentrate per serving with frozen fruit and your favorite dark green leafy vegetables. Add a little chilled Basic Manoomin Pudding (page 38) along with enough Manoomin Milk (page 37) to get the consistency you like, and sweeten to taste.

# Baby Yoda's Favorite Hot Choccy

**VEGAN, GLUTEN FREE**                                      Makes 4 cups

*Baby Yoda loves dried frog egg tea, but when he's visiting Earth he prefers dried fruit and herbal teas. Teas that aren't too acidic are best—such as blackberry leaf and dried elderberry—as a lot of acidity can curdle milk. Being lactose intolerant, Baby Yoda likes nondairy milk in his hot choccy. Baby Yoda likes to sprinkle Ginger Maple Sugar Manoomin Dust (page 122) on his hot choccy and pair it with Spiced Juneberry Muffins (page 125).*

¾ cup water
2 tea bags of choice (see note above)
2–4 tablespoons Dry-Toasted
   Manoomin (page 33)
¼ cup cocoa

¼ cup maple sugar
dash salt
dash cinnamon
3¼ cups milk of choice
dash vanilla extract, optional

Measure water in a large glass measuring cup and microwave for 2 minutes. Add tea bags and toasted manoomin either loose (will need to strain ) or in a tea ball. Let steep for a few minutes while you work on the cocoa mix.

In a large pot, whisk together cocoa, sugar, salt, and cinnamon. Remove tea bags (and strain out manoomin), then add tea to pot. Heat at medium, whisking regularly until everything is well blended. Add milk and heat just until hot. Add a dash of vanilla for serving if desired.

Easy Rustic Manoomin Cranberry Birch Bread

# Easy Rustic Manoomin Cranberry Birch Bread

**VEGETARIAN**  Makes 1 loaf

*This bread is soft and moist. You can make rolls instead of a loaf: separate dough into about half-cup portions and roll into balls. Make sure they have a little coating of oil and that their sides gently touch in the pan.*

1 cup warm water
1 packet (2¼ teaspoons) quick-rise yeast
2 teaspoons maple sugar
1 tablespoon birch syrup (or substitute maple syrup or sorghum)
2 tablespoons + 1 teaspoon oil

2½ cups + 4–5 tablespoons bread flour (or substitute all-purpose flour)
1 teaspoon salt
⅔ cup manoomin
⅓ cup dried cranberries

Heat oven to 350 degrees. Lightly grease a baking sheet or line with a silicone mat or parchment paper.

In a bowl, whisk together water, yeast, and maple sugar. Let sit until mixture bubbles up a bit (see tip). Stir in birch syrup and 2 tablespoons oil. In a separate bowl, mix together 2½ cups flour and salt, then slowly add yeast mixture. Mix dough with a wooden spoon, then stir in manoomin and cranberries. Turn dough out onto a lightly floured surface and begin kneading, sprinkling on more flour as needed to keep it from getting sticky. Knead for a few minutes: dough should bounce back when you poke it. Roll dough ball in 1 teaspoon oil in bowl, then sprinkle with flour and shape into a 2½x9–inch loaf on prepared baking sheet. Gently rub another pinch or two of flour onto the loaf. Let rise on warm stovetop for 4–5 minutes. Bake for 30–35 minutes or until deep golden brown. Cool, then slice and serve.

> **TIP:** In the middle of winter in Minnesota, it's hard to find a nice warm spot in my kitchen for yeast to work its magic. I like to put the bowl on top of my warm oven.

# Jalapeño Manoomin Yeast Rolls

Makes about 10 rolls

*Try adding ⅓ cup cooked manoomin to this recipe for extra manoomin power. For cheesy rolls, add ½ cup shredded cheese. You can adapt this recipe with baking powder instead of yeast and make biscuits instead of rolls. You can use this recipe for brat buns as well: just shape into 1½x6–inch cigars. They have some chew to them, which my husband seems to like.*

1 cup warm water
1 packet (2¼ teaspoons) quick-rise yeast
2 teaspoons maple sugar
3 cups all-purpose wheat flour or
    all-purpose gluten-free flour
¼ cup Manoomin Flour (page 35)
1 teaspoon salt

1 egg for dough + 1 egg for wash
1½ tablespoons + ½ teaspoon oil
2 tablespoons softened butter
1 jalapeño, minced (about 3 tablespoons)
3 cloves garlic, minced
    (about 1 tablespoon)

Heat oven to 350 degrees. Grease a baking sheet or line with parchment paper or a silicone mat.

In a large bowl, whisk together water, yeast, and maple sugar until combined. Let sit for 5 minutes on stovetop until foamy.

In a medium bowl, combine flours and salt. Pour yeast mixture into dry ingredients, add 1 egg, 1½ tablespoons oil, and butter, then stir 12 times. Stir in jalapeño and garlic. Turn dough onto a floured surface and knead 2 minutes, adding a little flour as needed to keep from sticking. Roll dough in remaining ½ teaspoon oil and knead a few times. Separate dough into roll-sized portions and place on prepared baking sheet with edges gently touching. Let rise on warm stovetop for 10 minutes. Beat remaining egg and brush onto rolls. Bake about 30 minutes or until golden brown.

Wheat flour is grown across vast swaths of land where bison once roamed. I try to use as little wheat flour as possible, with the hopes that one day the bison might return.

Jalapeño Manoomin Yeast Rolls, brat bun version. Delicious with bison manoomin brats.

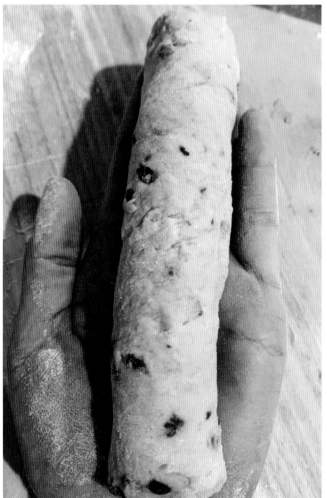

*Kristina Stanley, Ojibwe—Red Cliff Band of Lake Superior (see bio page 164)*

# Manoomin Seed Crackers

VEGAN, GLUTEN FREE                                    Makes about 3 dozen crackers

½ cup cooked wild rice
½ cup chia seeds
½ cup sunflower seeds
½ cup pumpkin seeds

¾–1 cup water
1½ teaspoons grated garlic
¼ teaspoon salt + more for sprinkling
oil

Heat oven to 300 degrees. Line baking sheets with parchment paper and brush lightly with oil.

In a large bowl, combine wild rice, chia seeds, sunflower seeds, and pumpkin seeds. Add the water, garlic, and salt and stir with a spatula until combined. Allow the mixture to sit until the chia seeds absorb the water and look like plump fish eggs, adding more water as needed. (Cover surface with plastic wrap if resting period is lengthy.)

Spread the mixture onto the prepared baking sheets. Brush top with oil. Place another piece of parchment over top and use a pastry roller to roll the cracker thin and even. Trim the edges with a pastry cutter. Brush again with oil if needed and sprinkle with salt.

Bake for 35 minutes. Remove from oven. If set enough to feel flexible, carefully cut into 4 pieces with pastry cutter. Flip the pieces, then cut each into 3x4-inch crackers. Bake for 25–35 minutes more, until lightly golden around the edges. Watch closely near the end to make sure they don't burn. Let cool completely on the pan. Store in an airtight container for up to 2 weeks.

Kevin Hart Jr. is a member of the Red Lake Band of Anishinaabe and is the frozen foods manager at the Red Lake Retail Center. He's also a fisherman, a hunter, and my dad. I love this recipe because it reminds me of the type of food I grew up eating: pure, delicious, and nutritious. In the winter, there's nothing like a bowl of hot brothy soup to warm your bones and fill your belly.

*Kevin Hart Jr.*

# Walleye Belly Soup

GLUTEN FREE                                                    Serves 12

*This recipe makes "enough to feed a small village."*

*On a fillet of walleye, you have your backs, tails, and bellies. Backs are often what you get at a restaurant if you order walleye "fingers." Bellies are less hefty and thinner than the other cuts. Be sure to cut out the line of bones in the walleye fillet when harvesting bellies for this soup. Cut bellies in half if they are large. A Red Laker can never have too much fish in a meal. Kevin recommends serving the other cuts of fish alongside this soup: dip fish in beaten eggs, roll in crushed saltines, and fry.*

4 quarts water
12 walleye bellies
   (about ½ pound)
1 cup wild rice
2 cups cooked hominy

3 potatoes,
   peeled and diced
2 small onions, diced
4 cloves garlic, minced
salt and pepper to taste

In a medium pot, add water, walleye bellies, wild rice, hominy, potatoes, onions, garlic, and salt and pepper. Bring to a boil, then reduce heat to medium. Cook until potatoes are soft, about 20 minutes.

**Awanigiizhik Bruce, Turtle Mountain Band
of Chippewa Indians of North Dakota (see bio page 115)**

# Wild Rice Blueberry Bison Stew

GLUTEN FREE                                                        Serves 15

*Boozhoo gakina awiya! Welcome everyone! This recipe was created with a fusion of my plains and woodland heritages in mind. I'm a Plains Ojibwe/Cree, and I wanted to make a dish with savory, sweet, and hardy flavor profiles like my ancestors would have for gatherings in the Turtle Mountain plateau, where I live.*

*This meal is versatile. You can substitute ingredients and make it to your own flavor profile. Maybe add some leeks, ramps, fiddleheads, or squash? Be creative and have fun! Please enjoy and make this recipe a family favorite from mine to yours.*

8 cups broth
3 cups wild rice
salt
splash soy sauce
splash maple syrup
1 red onion, diced
1 pound ground bison
garlic
thyme

rosemary
4–6 cups mixed frozen vegetables
    (potatoes, carrots, peas,
    beans, celery, etc.)
2–3 cups frozen blueberries
⅔ cup dried mixed berries
1 tablespoon cornstarch
splash wintergreen extract

In a Dutch oven or large pot, bring 8 cups broth to a boil. Add the wild rice. Season with salt, soy sauce, and maple syrup. Cover and simmer for 30–45 minutes, depending on the type of wild rice. Do not drain. Set aside to cool.

In a skillet, cook onion with bison, stirring to break up clumps. Season with garlic, thyme, rosemary, and salt. Drain out the grease. Add some broth and cook, stirring to scrape up browned bits from bottom of pan. Add bison to wild rice and set pot over medium heat.

Add vegetables, blueberries, and dried berries. After stew starts to simmer, stir in cornstarch and reduce heat. Stir in wintergreen extract and season to taste with rosemary, thyme, maple syrup, or salt. Enjoy your meal.

Miigwech sa dago mii'iw! Thank you and that's all!

*Awanigiizhik Bruce, Turtle Mountain Band of Chippewa Indians of North Dakota (see bio page 115)*

# Venison–Wild Rice Meat Loaf with Wild Plum–Tomato Coulis

Serves 12

*Boozhoo gakina awiya! Welcome everyone! This recipe was made during a holiday dinner a few years ago. Generally, I reserve my contemporary flair of traditional cooking for holidays with family and friends and our Native American ceremonies, festivals, and events. I love to Indigenize and fuse cultural flavors in my creative cooking processes. Within this dish I wanted to utilize flavor profiles of umami, savory, and sweet. Please enjoy and make this recipe a family favorite from mine to yours.*

## For coulis

2 tablespoons oil
1 onion, chopped
1–3 ribs celery, chopped
1–2 green bell peppers, chopped
2½ cups diced tomatoes
1–3 cups pitted wild plums
1 cup water
2 tablespoons honey
1 tablespoon marsala wine
1 tablespoon mirin
sprinkle cinnamon
sprinkle salt

## For meat loaf

4 cups water or broth + 1 cup water
2 cups wild rice
nori/seaweed
garlic
3–6 strips cooked bacon, crumbled
drizzle maple syrup
2 pounds ground venison
1 cup quick-cooking rolled oatmeal
1 cup flour
2–4 eggs or equivalent commodity dried egg mix
¼ cup oil
thyme
sage
tarragon
salt
pepper

To make the coulis, heat 2 tablespoons oil in a skillet and cook onions, celery, and green peppers until softened, stirring frequently. In a large pot, bring tomatoes, plums, and water to a boil. Add softened vegetables and stir in honey, marsala wine, mirin, cinnamon, and salt. Simmer over medium to low heat, stirring occasionally, until the sauce thickens. Remove from heat and allow sauce to cool. Place sauce into a blender or food processor and blend until mixture is smooth. Set aside.

To make meat loaf, heat oven to 350 degrees and grease a baking dish. In a large saucepan, bring 4 cups broth or water to a boil and add wild rice, nori, and garlic. Cover and simmer for 30–45 minutes, depending on the type of wild rice. Drain rice and mix in bacon and maple syrup. Set aside to cool and for flavors to meld.

In a large bowl, combine wild rice mixture, venison, oatmeal, flour, eggs (or egg mix), 1 cup water, oil, and seasonings to taste. Mix thoroughly. Place into prepared dish and shape into a meat loaf form. Top with most of the wild plum–tomato coulis, reserving some for serving. Bake for 1 hour or until loaf reaches internal temperature of 160 degrees.

Cool slightly before slicing. Drizzle with reserved coulis for final presentation. Enjoy your meal.

Miigwech sa dago mii'iw! Thank you and that's all!

Triple Chocolate Donuts

# Triple Chocolate Donuts

**VEGETARIAN, GLUTEN FREE**                    Makes 6 donuts

*If using cassava flour, the texture of these donuts will be a bit squishy while warm and will turn more wheat bread–like after completely cooled. I make them the night before and store the cooled donuts in an airtight container on the counter for a nice texture the next morning.*

**For the donuts**
½ cup cassava flour or flour
    of your choice
½ cup Manoomin Flour (page 35)
⅓ cup loosely packed maple sugar
3 tablespoons cocoa
½ teaspoon baking powder
½ teaspoon salt

1 egg
2 tablespoons oil
⅓ cup + 2 tablespoons Manoomin
    Milk (page 37)
½ teaspoon vanilla extract
¼ cup chocolate chips

**For the icing**
2 tablespoons cocoa
⅓ cup maple sugar
2 tablespoons Manoomin Milk (page 37)

Heat oven to 350 degrees and grease donut pan.

For the donuts, in a medium bowl, whisk together flours, maple sugar, cocoa, baking powder, and salt. In a separate bowl, beat egg and blend in oil, milk, and vanilla. Add wet ingredients to flour mixture and stir for about 30 seconds. Stir in chocolate chips.

Carefully pour or spoon the batter into individual molds in the prepared pan, filling up about three-quarters of the mold with batter and smoothing the top. Bake for 15–17 minutes or until a tester comes out clean.

Stir together icing ingredients until smooth, adding milk ½ tablespoon at a time. Let donuts cool slightly, then dip the tops into the icing and set aside to cool completely.

# Manoomin Hazelnut Bars

**VEGAN, GLUTEN FREE**                                    Makes 16 (2-inch) squares

*The pudding in these bars is enhanced in flavor and texture by the hazelnut milk. Delicious warm or chilled. Serve warm with your favorite fruit syrup or ice cream for a special treat.*

3 cups cooked manoomin
1 cup milk (hazelnut or other nondairy
    as desired) + extra as needed
½ cup + 3 tablespoons maple sugar

½ teaspoon salt
3 tablespoons crushed raw,
    unsalted hazelnuts
1–2 tablespoons maple or birch syrup

Heat oven to 350 degrees. Grease an 8x8–inch baking pan.

While manoomin is still warm, blend manoomin, milk, ½ cup maple sugar, and salt in a food processor until smooth and creamy. Some small pieces of manoomin may still be visible depending on the machine, but get the mixture as smooth as you can, adding a few tablespoons more milk as needed. Batter should be scoopable, not runny. Pour into prepared pan.

Bake 15 minutes and remove pan from oven. Insert a silicon spatula along the sides to press all of the edges away from the pan. Sprinkle remaining 3 tablespoons maple sugar to coat the top, then add hazelnuts and a pinch of salt. Drizzle 1–2 tablespoons maple or birch syrup on top and return pan to oven to bake another 12–15 minutes, or until the hazelnuts are toasted and fragrant. Remove from oven and cool slightly. Cut into bars with a silicone or nonstick spatula and serve.

Manoomin Hazelnut Bars

Using a mortar and pestle is a quick way to get a handful of crushed nuts to sprinkle on top.

# Manoomin Sweet Rolls Two Ways

VEGAN, GLUTEN-FREE OPTION                                   Makes about 12 rolls

*This recipe is meant to be exploratory. In my twenties, my favorite baking activity was to create a variety of interesting sweet rolls. You can make your sweet roll dough using a yeast dough or baking powder biscuit recipe: the choice is yours. If you choose a biscuit recipe, make sure it requires you to roll out the dough. You might want to try adding a little extra sweetness to your biscuit dough. Alter your chosen recipe to reflect a ratio of 3:1 all-purpose regular or gluten-free flour (or cassava, etc.) to Manoomin Flour (page 35). Essentially, you will substitute one-quarter of your flour for manoomin flour. After trying this ratio, you can alter the recipe to include more or less manoomin flour to suit your preferences.*

*For the sticky-sweet component, mix in a splash of Manoomin Milk (page 37) or dairy-free milk of choice with maple sugar, maple syrup, and a dash of salt in the following recipes to help replace the rich aspect of butter-laden sweet rolls. You will want your filling to be spreadable but with the consistency of a runny jam. If it's too runny, depending on the filling, you can add more maple sugar, cacao powder, or nut/seed butter to thicken it up. If it's too thick, add more maple syrup and/or milk of choice. The following are two suggested recipes to try. You can get creative with your sweet roll filling and add whatever you like.*

## Spicy Chocolate Rolls

Mix cocoa or cacao powder with maple sugar and blend with maple syrup and salt to taste. Include cinnamon or a little red chili paste for a cinnamon-chocolate-spicy flavor profile. Or leave out the spices altogether. Mixture should be sticky. Spread onto rolled-out dough, then tightly roll it up and cut into ¾- to 1-inch slices. Bake according to recipe instructions on silicone mat, parchment paper, or greased pan until lightly golden brown on edges. Cool and top with frosting or glaze of choice if desired.

## Wild Seed/Nut Caramel Rolls

Mix nut/seed butter with maple syrup and salt to taste. The seed/nut butter deepens the flavor and adds to the stickiness. Add spices if desired. Add milk and/or maple sugar if needed. Spread onto rolled-out dough, then tightly roll it up and cut into ¾- to 1-inch pieces. Bake according to recipe instructions on silicone mat, parchment paper, or greased pan until lightly golden brown on edges. Cool and top with frosting or glaze of choice if desired.

# Banana Manoomin Pie

*This pie has an interesting flavor profile that would be complemented with a drizzle of maple syrup and a sprinkle of Ginger Maple Sugar Manoomin Dust (page 122) just before serving, or caramel drizzle (see tip), or your favorite whipped topping. If you don't like banana, try using 1½ cups of pumpkin or other fruit puree instead.*

1 cup mashed banana
½ cup Basic Manoomin
    Pudding (page 38)
1¼ cups Manoomin Milk
    (page 37) or other milk
¼ cup maple sugar
¼ teaspoon nutmeg or cinnamon

½ teaspoon salt
3 eggs
¼ cup maple syrup
1 teaspoon vanilla
1 prebaked Manoomin Pie
    Crust (page 40)
fresh fruit: bananas, raspberries, etc.

Place banana, pudding, milk, maple sugar, nutmeg or cinnamon, and salt in a blender or food processor and blend until very smooth, with no lumps. The smoothness of your pudding will determine the smoothness of your pie. Transfer to a medium pot over low heat and whisk mixture for about 7–8 minutes. In a bowl, whisk together eggs and maple syrup, then whisk in the hot manoomin pudding mixture 1 tablespoon at a time, whisking continuously as you add it in. After at least 2 cups of pudding have been added to the bowl, whisk that mixture back into the pot. Continue to cook for 3–4 more minutes, whisking the pudding smooth as you go. Stir in vanilla.

Pour pudding into pie crust and top with banana slices, fresh whole raspberries, or any other fruit as desired. Allow to cool on the counter about 10 minutes, then cover tightly and chill pie in the refrigerator before serving. Keep pie covered for a crust that is soft and crumbly like a graham cracker crust. Leave pie uncovered for a crisp crust.

> **TIP:** To make caramel drizzle: whisk a couple tablespoons of maple sugar in a pot with just enough Manoomin Milk (page 37) for a runny, not watery, consistency. Add salt to taste and heat on medium-low, whisking constantly, until caramelly, about 5 minutes.

Manoomin Chocolate Pie

# Manoomin Chocolate Pie

**VEGETARIAN, GLUTEN FREE**                                      Makes 1 (9-inch) pie

*This is my absolute favorite pie. It's a chocolatey delight, but the manoomin pudding and eggs make it sit easier in the stomach than a chocolate pie made of mostly sugar, butter, and cream. Letting the pie chill, covered, in the refrigerator a couple hours ahead of serving is key to a nice balance of textures between the pudding and crust. Serve with fresh halved blackberries, whipped topping, chocolate shavings—whatever you want!*

1–2 cups Manoomin Maple
    Seed Mix (page 39)
½ cup Basic Manoomin
    Pudding (page 38)
½ cup Manoomin Milk (page 37)
1 cup maple sugar

3 tablespoons cocoa
2 eggs
1 teaspoon vanilla extract
½ teaspoon salt
¾ cup chopped semisweet chocolate

Heat oven to 350 degrees. Mix Manoomin Maple Seed Mix with water, 1 tablespoon at a time, until it sticks to itself; it won't take much. Grease a springform pan and press in seed dough. A thicker crust yields more chew; if you want a pie with an all-around smoother texture, press crust as thin as you can.

Whisk together pudding, milk, maple sugar, cocoa, eggs, vanilla, and salt until smooth, then transfer to a blender and add semisweet chocolate. Blend for 30 seconds, or until chocolate chunks are broken down. Pour batter into prepared crust. There will be small chocolate chunks at the bottom of the blender: be sure to spread them out evenly across the pie, where they will sink to the bottom.

Bake for 45 minutes. If your pie is raising in the middle after 30–40 minutes, just poke it with a fork and let it keep baking. Allow pie to cool on the counter about 10 minutes, then cover tightly and chill pie in the refrigerator before serving. Keep pie covered for a crust that is soft and crumbly like a graham cracker crust. Leave pie uncovered for a crisp crust.

# *Threads of Life:*
## Remembrance Is Sustenance

Everyone has something happen in their life that makes them ponder the mysterious nature of things. At two different times I have been visited by what I would call colorful strands of light. Both times they made themselves visible in a space that I can only describe as one that overlays typical reality.

The first time they made themselves known was during a long drive. I was in my twenties and in a lot of emotional pain. I used to call out for help a lot back then, often silently. As I was driving, the strands of light appeared in this in-between space. I could see in front of me both the road and also, on another level, the strands of light. They came down from above and ran right in front of me and then traveled way below me, extending farther in either direction than I could see. As I looked at them, I realized they were made up of life. My life. I could see all the moments in my life strung together in the strands. I looked down and saw things I had forgotten from my past. I saw things that reminded me why I was the way I was and how I had gotten to that moment. These reminders, some sad, some not, were overwhelming; it was so beautiful that I wept. I had to clench the steering wheel and bat the tears from my eyes.

The other time occurred when I was in my thirties and an observer at ceremony. After the ceremony it was nighttime at camp and people were in their tents. As I was lying down thinking about the day, the lights appeared again, strands of different colors, the same as the first time. Only now I did not see my own strands of lights but those of the people at camp. I could see through the tents that everyone had them, coming from the space above them and going through them. But one thing was different: in everyone's strands there were floating plates of food. These rectangular plates looked to be made of wood. The food looked like it was maybe cattail shoots—at least that was the closest thing I knew of at the time that resembled what was in the dishes.

Both of these occurrences give me hope and fill me with a feeling of remembrance and love that's like being held and told things by a grandparent who loves you very much. These strands of light and what they evoke is a form of sustenance that is not lost to time or distance or forgetfulness. It is always there. Moments of feeling loved like this have kept me going through the years. They also have inspired me to keep sending love into the universe in the dark times and to show gratitude for all the memories, new and old. I am always on the lookout for signs of the mysterious nature of how we are sustained by both memories and food. I think this sustenance might be one and the same.

# Resources and Recommended Reading ___

1854 Treaty Authority. "Biology of Wild Rice." www.1854treatyauthority.org/wild-rice/biology-of-wild-rice.html.

Child, Brenda. *Holding Our World Together: Ojibwe Women and the Survival of Community.* New York: Penguin, 2013.

Child, Brenda. *My Grandfather's Knocking Sticks: Ojibwe Family Life and Labor on the Reservation.* St. Paul: Minnesota Historical Society Press, 2014.

Dogan Abdulahad, Ismail Celik, and Mehmet Salih Kaya. "Antidiabetic Properties of Lyophilized Extract of Acorn (*Quercus brantii Lindl.*) on Experimentally STZ-Induced Diabetic Rats." *Journal of Ethnopharmacology* 176 (December 24, 2015): 243–51. doi: 10.1016/j.jep.2015.10.034.

Erdrich, Heid E. *Original Local: Indigenous Foods, Stories, and Recipes from the Upper Midwest.* St. Paul: Minnesota Historical Society Press, 2013.

Geniusz, Mary Siisip. *Plants Have So Much to Give Us, All We Have to Do Is Ask: Anishinaabe Botanical Teachings.* Edited by Wendy Makoons Geniusz. Illustrated by Annmarie Geniusz. Minneapolis: University of Minnesota Press, 2015.

Meeker, James E., Joan E. Elias, and John A. Heim. *Plants Used by the Great Lakes Ojibwa.* Odanah, WI: Great Lakes Indian Fish and Wildlife Commission, 1994.

Minnesota Department of Natural Resources. https://www.dnr.state.mn.us/.

Minnesota Wildflowers: A Field Guide to the Flora of Minnesota. www.minnesotawildflowers.info.

The Ojibwe People's Dictionary. University of Minnesota. https://ojibwe.lib.umn.edu.

Rao, Ankita. "Indigenous Women in Canada Are Still Being Sterilized Without Their Consent." VICE, September 9, 2019. https://tinyurl.com/vhuch24m.

The Rights of Manoomin. See Community Environmental Legal Defense Fund. "The Rights of Wild Rice." https://celdf.org/2019/02/the-rights-of-wild-rice/.

Thayer, Samuel. The Forager's Harvest website. https://www.foragersharvest.com.

Timoszuk, Magdalena, Katarzyna Bielawska, and Elżbieta Skrzydlewska. "Evening Primrose (*Oenothera biennis*) Biological Activity Dependent on Chemical Composition." *Antioxidants (Basel)* 7, no. 8 (2018): 108. doi: 10.3390/antiox7080108.

Photo by Ivy Vainio

# Index

Page references in *italics* indicate illustrations.

Tashia Hart is a culinary ethnobotanist, artist, photographer, writer, and cook. Her education in the field and in the kitchen began with a father who fishes, hunts, and harvests, a mom who cherishes plants, and a grandmother who was a career cook and baker. Hart has led foraging expeditions and developed recipes for Indigenous food–focused kitchens. Many of her talents are featured in this book: foraging tips, field photography, and creative recipes, all highlighting local flavors that celebrate the bounty of Minnesota fields, forests, and waters. She is Red Lake Anishinaabe. www.tashiahart.com

Photo by Jonathan Thunder

*The Good Berry Cookbook* was designed and set in type by Susan Everson in St. Paul, Minnesota. The typefaces are Circe and Acier. The book was printed by Versa Press in East Peoria, Illinois.